YORK NOTES

KT-493-573

HENRY V

WILLIAM SHAKESPEARE

NOTES BY DAVID LANGSTON

 Longman

 York Press

The right of David Langston to be identified as Author of this Work
has been asserted by him in accordance with the
Copyright, Designs and Patents Act 1988

YORK PRESS
322 Old Brompton Road, London SW5 9JH

PEARSON EDUCATION LIMITED
Edinburgh Gate, Harlow,
Essex CM20 2JE, United Kingdom
Associated companies, branches and representatives throughout the world

First published 1998
This new and fully revised edition first published 2003
Second impression 2003

10 9 8 7 6 5 4 3 2

ISBN 0-582-77268-0

Designed by Michelle Cannatella
Illustrations by Judy Stevens
Typeset by Pantek Arts Ltd, Maidstone, Kent
Produced by Pearson Education Asia Limited, Hong Kong

CONTENTS

PREFACE

York Notes are designed to give you a broader perspective on works of literature studied at GCSE and equivalent levels. With examination requirements changing in the twenty-first century, we have made a number of significant changes to this new series. We continue to help students to reach their own interpretations of the text but York Notes now have important extra-value new features.

You will discover that York Notes are genuinely interactive. The new **Checkpoint** features make sure that you can test your knowledge and broaden your understanding. You will also be directed to excellent websites, books and films where you can follow up ideas for yourself.

The **Resources** section has been updated and an entirely new section has been devoted to how to improve your grade. Careful reading and application of the principles laid out in the Resources section guarantee improved performance.

The **Detailed summaries** include an easy-to-follow skeleton structure of the story-line, while the section on **Language and style** has been extended to offer an in-depth discussion of the writer's techniques.

The Contents page shows the structure of this study guide. However, there is no need to read from the beginning to the end as you would with a novel, play or poem. Use the Notes in the way that suits you. Our aim is to help you with your understanding of the work, not to dictate how you should learn.

Our authors are practising English teachers and examiners who have used their experience to offer a whole range of **Examiner's secrets** – useful hints to encourage exam success.

The General Editor of this series is John Polley, Senior GCSE Examiner and former Head of English at Harrow Way Community School, Andover.

The author of these Notes is David Langston, who is an examiner for a major exam board. He has many years experience as an English teacher in High Schools and Colleges of Further Education and has written several study guides and English text books.

The text used in these Notes is The Arden Shakespeare *King Henry V*, edited by T.W. Craik (1995).

PART ONE

INTRODUCTION

HOW TO STUDY A PLAY

Though it may seem obvious, remember that a play is written to be performed before an audience. Ideally, you should see the play live on stage. A film or video recording is next best, though neither can capture the enjoyment of being in a theatre and realising that your reactions are part of the performance.

There are six aspects of a play:

1 THE PLOT: a play is a story whose events are carefully organised by the playwright in order to show how a situation can be worked out

2 THE CHARACTERS: these are the people who have to face this situation. Since they are human they can be good or bad, clever or stupid, likeable or detestable, etc. They may change too!

3 THE THEMES: these are the underlying messages of the play, e.g. jealousy can cause the worst of crimes; ambition can bring the mightiest low

4 THE SETTING: this concerns the time and place that the author has chosen for the play

5 THE LANGUAGE: the writer uses a certain style of expression to convey the characters and ideas

6 STAGING AND PERFORMANCE: the type of stage, the lighting, the sound effects, the costumes, the acting styles and delivery must all be decided

Work out the choices the dramatist has made in the first four areas, and consider how a director might balance these choices to create a live performance.

The purpose of these York Notes is to help you understand what the play is about and to enable you to make your own interpretation. Do not expect the study of a play to be neat and easy: plays are chosen for examination purposes, not written for them!

EXAMINER'S SECRET
It is really helpful to see performances of plays you are studying. For this play it would be good if you could see any of the preceding plays in the group: *Richard II, Henry IV, Part 1* and *Henry IV, Part 2.*

AUTHOR – LIFE AND WORKS

1564 William Shakespeare is baptised on 26 April in Stratford-on-Avon, Warwickshire

1582 Marries Anne Hathaway

1583 Birth of daughter, Susanna

1585 Birth of twins, Hamnet and Judith

1590–3 Early published works and poems written when theatres are closed by the Plague

1594 Joins Lord Chamberlain's Men (from 1603 named the King's Men) as actor and playwright

1595–9 Writes the history plays and comedies, including *Henry V*

1597 Shakespeare buys New Place, the second biggest house in Stratford

1599 Moves to newly-opened Globe Theatre

1599–1608 Writes his greatest plays, including *Macbeth*, *King Lear* and *Hamlet*

1608–13 Takes over the lease of Blackfriars Theatre and writes final plays, the romances, ending with *The Tempest*

1609 Shakespeare's sonnets published

1613 Globe Theatre burns down 29 June, during performance of *Henry VIII*

1616 Shakespeare dies, 23 April, and is buried in Stratford

1623 First Folio of Shakespeare's plays published

CONTEXT

1558 Elizabeth I becomes Queen of England

1568 Mary Queen of Scots is imprisoned for life

1577–80 Sir Francis Drake becomes the first to circumnavigate the world

1587 Mary Queen of Scots is executed

1588 Defeat of the Spanish Armada

1591 Tea is first drunk in England

1593–4 Outbreak of the Plague in London, closing theatres and killing as many as 5,000, according to some sources

1594 Queen Elizabeth spends Christmas at Greenwich and is entertained by leading theatre company of her day, headed by James Burbage, William Kempe and Shakespeare

1595 Walter Raleigh sails to Guiana

1599 Oliver Cromwell is born

1603 Elizabeth I dies on 24 March; James I, son of Mary, succeeds to throne of England

1604 Peace treaty signed with Spain

1605 The Gunpowder Plot

1611 The Bible is translated into the Authorised (King James) Version

1614 Fire sweeps through Stratford but New Place is spared

1618 Thirty Years War begins

SETTING AND BACKGROUND

THE HISTORICAL PERSPECTIVE

The monarchy

- Shakespeare deals with 'kingship' and the position of the monarchy in several of his plays.

- At the time Henry V was written there was a military campaign against the Irish which raised patriotic feelings in England.

For several hundred years the position of the monarch was seen as one ordained and approved by God. By Shakespeare's time certainties about the God-given order of things were being seriously challenged. The Protestant Reformation had rejected the authority of the Pope and his position as God's representative on earth. The increasingly numerous wealthy merchants were beginning to resent the privileges of the aristocracy.

Queen Elizabeth I reigned from 1558 to 1603. During the later years of her rule, when Shakespeare was writing his history plays, there were constant fears of plots and rebellions. Although Protestantism was the officially approved religion, there were pressures from Protestant extremists who wished to make further reforms, such as the removal of bishops. The existence of a large Catholic minority was also seen as a threat to the established order. Both factions were exploited by agents of foreign powers.

> **DID YOU KNOW?**
> After the defeat of the Spanish Armada in 1588 there was an increase in patriotic feeling in the country.

The importance of a stable monarchy

The issues of stable and legitimate monarchy, rank and order in society, unity, loyalty, rebellion and treason are significant themes in a number of Shakespeare's plays of this period. They were vitally relevant to the times. In *Henry V* we see the King check the legitimacy of his rights to France, act firmly on those rights, deal with treachery, unite and inspire his people and maintain a firm and just control.

Essex in Ireland

When *Henry V* was first performed, the Earl of Tyrone had recently led a rebellion against the English forces in Ireland. Queen Elizabeth appointed the popular Earl of Essex as governor of Ireland and he set off to suppress the rebels. There is a reference to his expected victorious return at the beginning of Act V, lines 29–32 (Chorus). Although the play is based on historical sources and is the completion of a series which begins with *Richard II*, we can see the parallel with the contemporary expedition to reclaim what was considered to be the monarch's rightful domain. Henry goes to France to claim his rights and Essex goes to Ireland to do the same on behalf of the Queen.

Shakespeare's sources

The main source used by Shakespeare for the events in *Henry V* was *Chronicles of England, Scotland and Ireland* by Raphael Holinshed, first published in 1577. He also used *The Union of the Two Noble* and *Illustre Families of Lancaster and York* written by Edward Hall and published in 1548, and an anonymous play, *The Famous Victories of Henry the Fifth*. Although the play follows some of Holinshed's detail closely, Shakespeare gives the story life and shape through his verse and dramatic invention.

Lowlife

In the sixteenth century, the population of London grew from 50,000 to 200,000, despite a serious outbreak of plague. It was a centre of trade and commerce and also a focus for those who wished to find favour at court. At the other end of the social scale it was home to a large criminal underclass of thieves, professional beggars, swindlers, prostitutes, pimps and brothel-keepers.

In *Henry IV, Part 1* and *Part 2*, Shakespeare shows us his familiarity with this underworld through his amusing portraits of the lowlife characters. Some of these characters survive in *Henry V* and see the military campaign as an opportunity to extend their thieving into new pastures.

DID YOU KNOW?

Essex was cheered by the people of London as he left for Ireland.

CHECK THE NET

You can learn quite a lot about London in the sixteenth century on the Internet.

The theatre

By the time *Henry V* was performed, the theatre in London was well established but operated under some difficulties. The court welcomed new drama and patronised the playwrights and players, but the Puritan local authorities disapproved. They considered plays and play-acting to be immoral and they believed that the playhouses attracted criminals and encouraged lewd behaviour. Public performances were usually held outside the city boundaries in inn yards and later in purpose-built theatres like the Globe. The profession of acting was not recognised in law and actors could be treated as vagabonds who had no visible means of support. It was therefore important that they came under the patronage and protection of powerful people.

EXAMINER'S SECRET

You will gain more credit if you show you have some understanding of the play in its historical context.

Now take a break!

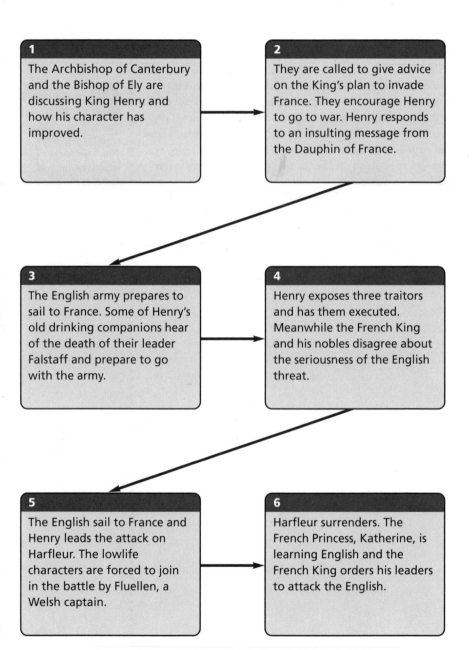

1

The Archbishop of Canterbury and the Bishop of Ely are discussing King Henry and how his character has improved.

2

They are called to give advice on the King's plan to invade France. They encourage Henry to go to war. Henry responds to an insulting message from the Dauphin of France.

3

The English army prepares to sail to France. Some of Henry's old drinking companions hear of the death of their leader Falstaff and prepare to go with the army.

4

Henry exposes three traitors and has them executed. Meanwhile the French King and his nobles disagree about the seriousness of the English threat.

5

The English sail to France and Henry leads the attack on Harfleur. The lowlife characters are forced to join in the battle by Fluellen, a Welsh captain.

6

Harfleur surrenders. The French Princess, Katherine, is learning English and the French King orders his leaders to attack the English.

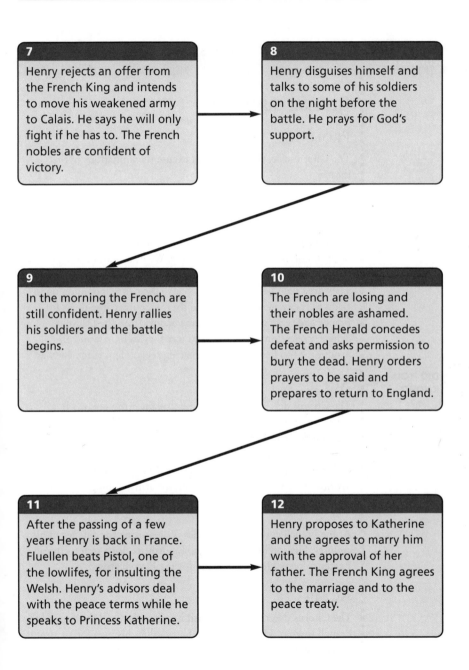

7

Henry rejects an offer from the French King and intends to move his weakened army to Calais. He says he will only fight if he has to. The French nobles are confident of victory.

8

Henry disguises himself and talks to some of his soldiers on the night before the battle. He prays for God's support.

9

In the morning the French are still confident. Henry rallies his soldiers and the battle begins.

10

The French are losing and their nobles are ashamed. The French Herald concedes defeat and asks permission to bury the dead. Henry orders prayers to be said and prepares to return to England.

11

After the passing of a few years Henry is back in France. Fluellen beats Pistol, one of the lowlifes, for insulting the Welsh. Henry's advisors deal with the peace terms while he speaks to Princess Katherine.

12

Henry proposes to Katherine and she agrees to marry him with the approval of her father. The French King agrees to the marriage and to the peace treaty.

PART TWO

SUMMARIES

GENERAL SUMMARY

PROLOGUE

The Chorus asks the audience to excuse the limitations of the theatre.

ACT I

The Archbishop of Canterbury and the Bishop of Ely are concerned about a proposed bill which would transfer a great deal of the Church's property to the King. We hear that the King's character has greatly improved since he has come to the throne. They are called before the King to give their expert opinion on his claim to the crown of France and they encourage him to go to France and seize what is his. Ambassadors from the Dauphin deliver a rejection of his claims to territory in France and an insulting gift. Henry sends a menacing reply. He is ready for war.

 DID YOU KNOW?

Henry IV, Part 1 and *Henry IV, Part 2* are plays that feature Henry V as a youth.

ACT II

The Chorus describes the excitement as the army gets ready to depart from Southampton. We witness a quarrel between some of the lowlife characters in London and learn that Sir John Falstaff is ill. At Southampton, King Henry exposes three traitors and sentences them to death. Meanwhile Falstaff has died and the lowlife characters are leaving to join the army, hoping to profit from the war.

At the French court, King Charles is organising the defence of his country. His son believes that the English are not a serious threat. Exeter delivers Henry's demand for the French crown.

ACT III

The Chorus describes the English invasion fleet and the siege of the French town of Harfleur. King Henry rallies his men for an assault on Harfleur. He persuades the Governor of Harfleur to surrender.

At the French court, Princess Katherine tries to learn some English from her maid. The French King discusses Henry's progress with his nobles. He orders them to move against the English and sends a herald to Henry with terms for his surrender and ransom. Henry says that he does not wish to fight but will do so. The night before battle, the French nobles boast to each other about their equipment and horses.

ACT IV

The Chorus describes the scene as the two armies wait for the morning. King Henry moves round the camp visiting his men in disguise. In the morning the French nobles, full of confidence, leave their camp for the battlefield.

Henry addresses his leaders, saying that the day will go down in history and that those who stayed in England will always regret that they were not present at the battle. He urges his men forward.

We are shown a number of short scenes from the battle: Pistol captures a French soldier; the French nobles are shocked and ashamed by their lack of success; the French herald comes to concede defeat and to ask Henry's permission to gather the dead.

ACT V

The Chorus tells us of Henry's enthusiastic reception in London. He then asks us to skip over the intervening events and, like Henry, return to France. Fluellen takes revenge on Pistol for insulting him. King Henry and his nobles meet with the French. Henry leaves his advisors to discuss the peace terms while he talks to Princess Katherine and wins her consent to be his wife. The King of France agrees to the terms and to his daughter's marriage to King Henry.

EPILOGUE

The Chorus closes with an apology for the shortcomings of the drama. We are told that King Henry's gains were lost in the reign of his son Henry VI.

CHECK THE FILM

Chimes at Midnight (Orson Welles, 1966) is a wonderful compendium of *Henry IV, Part 1* and *Part 2*. It covers the events of Henry V's youth and his association with Falstaff and the other rogues. Orson Welles is brilliant as Falstaff. The film is particularly helpful in understanding the background to *Henry V*.

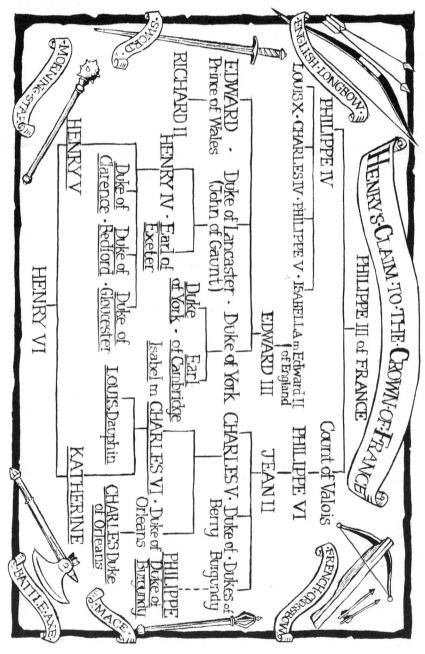

Henry's Claim to the Crown of France

PHILIPPE III of FRANCE

PHILIPPE IV	Count of Valois
LOUIS X · CHARLES IV · PHILIPPE V · ISABELLA m Edward II of England	PHILIPPE VI
EDWARD III	JEAN II
EDWARD · Duke of Lancaster · Duke of York	CHARLES V · Duke of · Dukes of
Prince of Wales (John of Gaunt)	Berry Burgundy
RICHARD II	
HENRY IV · Earl of Duke Earl	Isabel m CHARLES VI · Duke of
Exeter of York · of Cambridge	Orleans Orleans
HENRY V Duke of Duke of	LOUIS, Dauphin CHARLES, Duke PHILIPPE, Duke of
Clarence · Bedford · Gloucester	of Orleans Burgundy
HENRY VI	KATHERINE

DETAILED SUMMARIES

CHORUS – Introduction

1 **The Chorus introduces the play.**

2 **He encourages the audience to use their imagination.**

The play opens with a Prologue spoken by the Chorus. The Chorus was used in classical Greek drama to comment on the action and usually consisted of a group of actors. In this play, the Chorus is spoken by a single actor. He calls for inspiration to help show the great events and heroic characters involved in the story which is to be presented. He asks the audience to make allowances for the limitations of the small theatre, 'this wooden O' (line 13), and encourages them to use their imaginations to conjure up the 'two mighty monarchies' (line 20) and the large number of men and horses involved in the battles.

Shakespeare wishes to impress his audience that this is an epic story they are about to see and he enlists their help in its creation.

CHECKPOINT 1

Why 'this wooden O'?

CHECKPOINT 2

What 'two mighty monarchies'?

 CHECK THE FILM

In Kenneth Branagh's film, *Henry V* (1989), Sir John Gielgud as the Chorus asks the audience to excuse the limitations of the film studio rather than the theatre.

SCENE 1 – A reformed man

❶ Two religious leaders discuss the King.

❷ They comment on the improvement in Henry's character.

CHECK THE FILM

Laurence Olivier's version of *Henry V* (1945) was released in wartime and its patriotic message seemed very appropriate. It is set partly in a representation of Shakespeare's theatre and partly on location. Olivier gives a very powerful performance in the role of Henry.

The Archbishop of Canterbury and the Bishop of Ely are discussing the reintroduction of a government bill which will strip the Church of a great deal of its wealth. The Archbishop takes some comfort in the fact that the King seems to be in sympathy with them and has been offered a substantial gift of money.

We hear that the King's character has reformed since he has come to the throne, 'full of grace and fair regard' (line 22), and that he is widely admired and respected for his scholarship and his skill in debate.

Henry's wild youth

The description of the changes in King Henry's character reminds the audience of his wild and reckless behaviour as Prince Hal in the previous two plays in the series, *Henry IV, Part 1* and *Part 2*. The audience will be interested to see this reformed King living up to the promises he made in *Henry IV, Part 1* (Act I, Scene 2).

The Archbishop also mentions the King's claims to, 'the crown and seat of France' (line 88) and the presence of French Ambassadors at the court.

CHECKPOINT 3

Why are the churchmen keen on the King's proposed invasion of France?

We see that the churchmen have a strong motive for encouraging the King's claims in France. If they finance the war, it will turn attention away from the bill which has been proposed.

The main plot of the King's claim to the crown of France is introduced and we anticipate the confrontation between Henry and the French Ambassadors.

SCENE 2 – France insults England

① **Henry seeks Church backing for his war in France.**

② **He considers the danger of the Scots taking advantage of his absence to invade England.**

③ **The Dauphin sends Henry an insulting message.**

King Henry sends for the Archbishop of Canterbury and asks him for his considered opinion on his legal rights to his claims in France. He warns the Archbishop that a great deal of blood may be shed as a consequence of his advice and he must take care how he awakes the 'sleeping sword of war' (line 22).

The Archbishop gives a detailed history of the kingdoms of France and Germany. He argues that the Salic law, which excludes succession through the female line and which has been used by the French to deny Henry's claim, is valid only in Germany and does not apply in France.

Henry asks the Archbishop to confirm his right to make the claim, which he does, reminding him of his ancestors' victories against the French and promising a generous donation from the Church.

King Henry wants religious and legal support for his claim. He makes the Archbishop share the responsibility for the proposed war.

The Archbishop gives his legal opinion but also encourages Henry with references to his heroic ancestors. Both the Archbishop and the Bishop of Ely speak of, 'blood and sword and fire' (line 131).

Some of the nobles present add their encouragement. The King then considers the possibility that the Scots may take advantage of his absence which shows that he is a cautious and responsible ruler. The Archbishop, using as a metaphor the diverse but cooperative functions of bees in a bee-hive, suggests that the King divides his forces into four and takes one quarter with him to France. Henry says he is determined to rule France or to die in the attempt.

CHECK THE FILM

Kenneth Branagh's production of *Henry V* (1989) attempts greater realism in the battle scenes and focuses more on Henry's inner conflicts. There is not as much emphasis on the patriotic elements of the play as in Olivier's version. Branagh himself gives an excellent performance in the lead role.

DID YOU KNOW?

Some of the most effective soldiers fighting for the King of France were Scottish mercenaries.

CHECKPOINT 4

What danger may threaten England while Henry is away in France?

CHECKPOINT 5

How has
Shakespeare
reduced the force
of the Dauphin's
comments about
Henry?

The French Ambassadors are shown in. They are from the Dauphin, son of the French King. Henry assures them that they may speak plainly. The Dauphin's message is an insulting rejection of Henry's claims to French dukedoms and contains references to the English King's former reputation as a trivial pleasure-seeker. This message is accompanied by a mocking gift of tennis balls.

The significance of the tennis balls

King Henry, showing dignity, self-control and wit, takes up the theme of tennis in his reply and warns that a deadly game will follow, 'this mock of his / Hath turned his balls to gun-stones' (lines 283–4). He says that his life so far has merely been preparation for taking his place on the throne of France. The Dauphin's mockery will bring much misery and hardship on the French people as Henry intends to proceed in a just and, 'well-hallowed' (line 294) cause. There is a cold, menacing determination in his speech. Henry turns the Dauphin's tennis balls back in his face.

When the Ambassadors are dismissed Henry tells his followers to direct all their energies to preparing the expedition.

We are given the impression of nobles and Church being united behind an intelligent and formidable young monarch.

GLOSSARY

gun-stones cannon
balls

well-hallowed blessed
holy

 Now take a break!

WHO SAYS?

1 'If it pass against us / We lose the better half of our possession'

....

6 'We'll chide this Dauphin at his father's door'

....

2 'May I with right and conscience make this claim?'

....

5 'This was a merry message'

....

3 'Awake remembrance of these valiant dead, / And with your puissant arm renew their feats'

....

4 'There's naught in France / That can be with a nimble galliard won'

....

ABOUT WHOM?

7 '... his addiction was to courses vain, / His companies unlettered, rude, and shallow'

....

8 '... this mock of his / Hath turned his balls to gun-stones'

....

Check your answers on page 75.

CHORUS – Preparations

❶ England prepares for war.

❷ King Henry is in danger in his own country.

The Chorus tells us about the excitement and anticipation in England as the King and his followers prepare for war. 'Now all the youth of England are on fire' (line 1). We learn that the French have bribed three English traitors, 'corrupted men' (line 22), to murder Henry before he sets sail. This will arouse the curiosity of the audience. When we next see the King he will be in Southampton.

The business-like preparations of the English contrast with the vanity and show of the French nobles later in the play.

SCENE 1 – Henry's old life slips away

❶ Henry's old drinking companions fall out amongst themselves.

❷ Sir John Falstaff is very ill.

Bardolph and Nym, two of the old drinking companions of King Henry's youth, meet and discuss Nym's quarrel with Pistol, another lowlife character. Pistol is married to Nell Quickly, hostess of a tavern, who had previously been engaged to Nym. These three rogues call each other by military ranks as they are about to set off, 'all three sworn brothers' (line 12), on the expedition to France.

> ### Henry's former companions
>
> The lowlife characters bring humour to the play and their scenes provide light relief from the serious events of the main plot. They also remind the audience of the King's wild youth and serve to underline the great changes in his behaviour and bearing.

When Pistol enters with his wife, he and Nym exchange extravagant and ludicrous insults and threaten to fight each other. Bardolph comes between them. Pistol speaks in a bombastic, comical kind of

DID YOU KNOW?

The Catholic kingdom of Spain was England's main enemy during the reign of Queen Elizabeth I, and Catholics in England were treated with suspicion.

DID YOU KNOW?

Early English verse was heavily alliterative so Shakespeare is making fun of an old-fashioned style here.

verse. It is a windy parody of **epic** style, full of **alliteration** and suits his boastful, empty bravado.

A boy servant enters with news that his master is very ill and begs them to come to him. (His master is Sir John Falstaff – another of the King's old drinking companions now cast off by the reformed and responsible monarch.) The Hostess leaves with the Boy and Bardolph establishes a truce between Pistol and Nym. The Hostess returns and begs them to come to the sick Sir John. It is suggested that he is suffering from a broken heart because of the King's treatment of him. '**The King hath killed his heart**' (line 88).

CHECK THE FILM

Falstaff does not actually appear in this play although he is shown in Kenneth Branagh's (1989) film of *Henry V*.

SCENE 2 – The army prepares

1 **Henry shows mercy and strength.**

2 **Henry believes God is on his side.**

Some of the English lords are discussing the villainy of the traitors in their midst when the King enters in the company of the three conspirators. He asks their opinion of the prospects for his invasion of France. They answer with encouraging words and he says he will not forget to reward people according to their deserts.

Henry orders the release of a drunk who was arrested for shouting insults about him in the streets, but the traitors protest that he is being too lenient. He then hands the traitors written orders which are in fact details of their treachery. Henry shows his command of the situation by playing with the traitors. They immediately fall on their knees and submit to his mercy. Henry tells them, 'The mercy that was quick in us but late / By your own counsel is suppressed and killed' (lines 79–80). He denounces them for their treason, particularly Lord Scroop, that 'savage and inhuman creature' (line 95), who had been close to him and in whom he had confided a great deal. We see that Henry is firm in his punishment of serious crimes and confident enough be merciful in the case of the drunk.

CHECKPOINT 6

What other possible dangers has Henry had to consider?

Treachery

The traitors repent and accept their fate. King Henry sentences them to death and they are taken away to be executed. The discovery of the plot is seen by Henry as a sign that God is on his side and he orders the immediate departure of the invasion fleet: 'Cheerly to sea; the signs of war advance' (line 193).

SCENE 3 – The footsoldiers prepare

❶ **Henry's old drinking partners prepare to go to war.**

This scene provides another short relief from the serious action. Pistol, Bardolph, Nym and the Boy are leaving London to join the army. Pistol's wife, the Hostess, is seeing them off and she gives a pathetic and comic account of the death of Falstaff.

The death of Falstaff

Falstaff's death marks the end of an era. He was the leader and the inspiration of this band of thieves and rogues.

Pistol warns her to take good care of business. The rogues leave for France with the intention of profiting from the war. Pistol's image of going to France to suck blood, 'like horse-leeches, my boys,' (line 53) is a suitable one as they intend to be parasites and steal what they can.

SCENE 4 – The French misjudge Henry

❶ **The Dauphin is headstrong and overconfident.**

❷ **The French King is cautious.**

The King Charles orders his nobles and his son to strengthen the defences against the English invasion. The Dauphin agrees that precautions should be taken but refuses to accept that the English King is a serious threat, dismissing him as, 'a vain, giddy, shallow, humorous youth,' (line 28).

French misjudgements

The French King brushes aside a warning from the Constable of France who believes that Henry has changed. His father, the King, treats the invasion as a grave danger and refers to previous English successes. He is cautious and weak and does not inspire his followers. Instead he talks of fears and old defeats. We see here the first signs of disunity among the French. We are also reminded that Henry has cast off his previous idle ways. This builds up our anticipation to see him in action.

CHECKPOINT 7

In what ways is the French court different from the English?

GLOSSARY

horse-leeches large blood-sucking worms

humorous fickle

Scene 4 continued

CHECKPOINT 8

What is the great contrast between Henry and the French King as seen here?

The Duke of Exeter arrives as Ambassador for King Henry. He demands that Charles surrenders, 'the borrowed glories' (line 79) of the crown of France and he hands him a family tree which proves the justice of Henry's claim. Refusal will bring about great suffering and death. King Charles says he will give his answer on the following day.

CHECK THE BOOK

An A.B.C. of Shakespeare, Peter Bayley (Longman York Handbooks), is a useful resource.

Exeter then tells the Dauphin that King Henry wishes him to know that he will regret his insulting gift and delivers a message of, 'Scorn and defiance, slight regard, contempt' (line 117).

Exeter is bold and confident. Unlike the French Ambassadors, he does not hesitate to deliver his message.

Now take a break!

Who says?

1 'For now sits expectation in the air'

....

5 'Good my sovereign, / Take up the English short and let them know / Of what a monarchy you are the head'

....

2 'O braggart vile and damned furious wight, / The grave doth gape, and doting death is near'

....

4 'Our purposes God justly hath discovered, / And I repent my fault more than my death'

....

3 'Enlarge the man committed yesterday / That railed against our person'

....

About whom?

6 'That he should for a foreign purse so sell / His sovereign's life to death and treachery!'

....

8 'a vain, giddy, shallow, humorous youth'

....

7 'Nay, sure, he's not in hell; he's in Arthur's bosom, if ever a man went to Arthur's bosom'

....

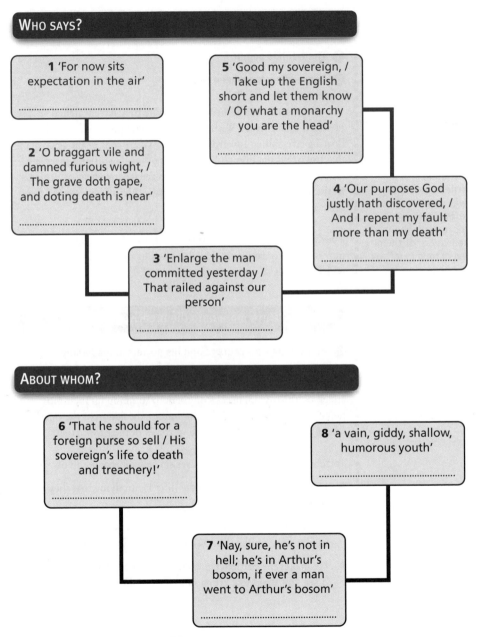

Check your answers on page 75.

Chorus – War

1 **The war has begun.**

2 **Peace offers have been rejected.**

The Chorus asks the audience to imagine they have watched Henry's, 'brave fleet / With silken streamers' (lines 5–6) like a floating city, sailing towards Harfleur. We are told of the siege of that town and the French King's offer of his daughter in marriage together with some dukedoms. This is the first we hear of Princess Katherine and the suggestion of marriage. Henry has rejected the offer and the siege continues.

The Chorus is used to help create the sense of spectacle and the movement of great forces. He also gives us historical information which helps us to understand later events.

Scene 1 – 'Once more unto the breach, dear friends'

1 **Henry shows his courage and his powers of leadership.**

At the siege of Harfleur, King Henry rallies his men for one more attack on the town. He calls on them to summon up their most fierce and aggressive qualities, to 'imitate the action of the tiger' (line 6) and reminds them of the victories of their forefathers.

To achieve his purpose Henry uses several approaches in his speech:

- He calls his men 'dear friends' (line 1), implying that they are his willing companions.

- He flatters the ordinary soldiers (yeomen) with the suggestion that he sees 'noble' (line 30) qualities shining in their eyes.

- He makes the battle seem exciting by comparing it to a hunt. 'I see you stand like greyhounds in the slips' (line 31).

> **The power of oratory**
>
> Great leaders throughout history have been able to move men by the power of their speeches. Henry may be an early example but the similar ability is evident through the ages.
>
> Mark Antony, in the play *Julius Caesar*, brings the crowd in Rome to his side by the brilliance of his speech that begins, 'Friends, Roman, countrymen...'. In more modern times we have only to look at the opposing leaders of Britain and Germany during the Second World War, Hitler and Sir Winston Churchill to see how their rhetoric inspired their nations.

SCENE 2 – Lowlife humour

❶ Comic relief is provided by the lowlife characters.

❷ Bardolph, Nym and Pistol are worthless as soldiers.

❸ We meet Captain Fluellen.

Bardolph leads the lowlife characters at the tail-end of the attack, but Nym, Pistol and the Boy are reluctant to go any further. Fluellen, a Welsh captain, arrives and drives the three rogues forward 'Up to the breach you dogs!' (line 21). The Boy is left on stage. We feel sympathy for him as he says that he is tired of working for such cowards and thieves and he plans to find better employment.

Fluellen returns and meets Gower, an English captain. They discuss the progress of the mines which are being dug to blow up the town walls. Fluellen expresses contempt for captain Macmorris, an Irishman, who is in charge of the work: 'he is an ass, as any is in the world' (lines 70–1). Macmorris arrives with captain Jamy, a Scotsman, and a comical discussion follows. Captain Gower is trying to keep the peace between Fluellen and Macmorris when they are interrupted by the sound of a trumpet-call from the town.

EXAMINER'S SECRET

Spend most time on the questions that offer most marks.

CHECKPOINT 9

What are the nationalities represented by the captains?

EXAMINER'S SECRET
Good details are as effective as direct quotations.

The amusement of dialects and accents

Shakespeare's audience would have found the language of the captains amusing. They are national stereotypes. The fact that they are having a serious dispute about the technical aspects of warfare in their comic dialects adds to the humour.

The presence of English, Irish, Scots and Welsh captains suggests a broad base of British support for Henry which is not historically sound, but reflects the political circumstances of Shakespeare's time. The captains take their work seriously and are loyal soldiers.

SCENE 3 – Henry takes Harfleur

❶ **Henry is successful at Harfleur.**

❷ **He paints a fearsome picture of the sack of the town.**

King Henry addresses the Governor of Harfleur. He tells him that this is his last chance to surrender and describes in vivid terms the destruction and murder, 'waste and desolation' (line 18), which will follow if the English troops are let loose in the town. The Governor has been told that the Dauphin is unable to send him reinforcements and he surrenders.

The horrors of war

All wars involve bloodshed and suffering and such scenes may harden a soldier. Henry, however, is seen to be both merciful towards the French people and careful with his own troops. He avoids unnecessary bloodshed. In his speech we are given a graphic description of the brutalities of warfare.

The King leaves Exeter in charge of the town with instructions to be merciful to the people. His army has been weakened and with, 'winter coming on and sickness growing,' (line 55) he intends to withdraw to Calais for the winter.

We learn that despite this victory the English army is weak and vulnerable. The French have not yet committed their main forces.

SCENE 4 – Romance in the air

❶ Princess Katherine tries to learn English.

Speaking in French, the Princess Katherine asks her maid to teach her English. The maid, whose command of English is very poor, tells her the names of parts of the body and Katherine tries to memorise them. Some of the English words sound rather indecent to French ears and the Princess is shocked.

CHECKPOINT 10

What other examples have we had of Henry's trust in Exeter?

EXAMINER'S SECRET
Keep an eye on the clock so that you do not run out of time.

CHECKPOINT 11

Why does Princess Katherine want to learn English?

The amusement of language

The audience would be amused to hear the French characters mispronouncing English words. Even in Shakespeare's day it was easy to raise a laugh at the expense of 'funny' foreigners and their inability to speak correct English.

Those in the audience who understood French would be more amused by the Princess's response to the English words, 'coun' ('gown') and 'foot' (line 46), which sounded like coarse and indelicate expressions in her own language.

The humour derived from Katherine's struggle to speak English defuses some of the grimness the audience has just felt having been confronted with the horrors of war.

EXAMINER'S SECRET

The answer booklet contains enough paper for you to get top marks!

We have heard about Katherine as a possible bride for Henry. We now see that she is a lively good-humoured young woman.

SCENE 5 – French contempt for the English

❶ The French continue to underestimate the English.

The Dauphin and the French nobles are eager to attack the English. They are angry and insulted by the presence of Henry's troops and express contempt for the, 'foggy, raw and dull' (line 16) little island they have come from. According to the Dauphin the French ladies have begun to mock their menfolk for their lack of courage.

CHECKPOINT 12

What is ironic about the French attitude towards the English?

The French King orders his nobles to attack the English and to capture Henry but refuses to allow the Dauphin to go with the army. The Constable of France regrets that, because the English army is so small and weak, Henry will probably surrender without a fight. The French despise the English and consider their royalty to be an illegitimate offshoot of France: 'Norman bastards' (line 10).

> **French attitudes towards the English**
>
> The French describe the country and the climate in insulting terms. The audience will be eager to see them humbled.
>
> The French use casual oaths in their conversation unlike Henry who is pious and dignified in his speech.
>
> King Charles's list of the French nobility who are to attack the English is echoed later in the list of the dead and prisoners after Agincourt (Act IV, Scene 8).

SCENE 6 – Henry is defiant

❶ **Bardolph has come to the end of his criminal career.**

❷ **Henry refuses to be ransomed. He will die with his men if he is defeated.**

Fluellen meets captain Gower and tells him about some fighting he has been involved in, defending a bridge with the Duke of Exeter. He says that he noted the bravery of one particular man in the action. This turns out to be Pistol who arrives to ask Fluellen to go to the Duke of Exeter and intercede for Bardolph who is about to be hanged for stealing from a church. Fluellen believes, 'discipline ought to be used' (line 55) and refuses to interfere. Pistol curses him and leaves. Gower says he recognises Pistol for a well-known rogue, 'an arrant counterfeit rascal' (line 60) and the kind of man who will return to England and live off his tales of the war. Fluellen agrees that Pistol has deceived him.

King Henry enters and Fluellen reports the Duke of Exeter's successful action at the bridge. When asked about English casualties Fluellen says that the only loss is a man called Bardolph, about to be hanged for theft. Even though this was one of his old companions Henry expresses his approval. He 'would have all such offenders so cut off' (line 106), and orders that there is to be no theft from or abuse of the French people. Fluellen's report of the action at the

CHECKPOINT 13

Who are Bardolph's companions?

 **EXAMINER'S SECRET**

You will gain marks if you can make comparisons, such as between Henry and the Dauphin.

bridge helps to give the impression of a moving campaign and the feeling that the audience is seeing part of a larger series of events.

EXAMINER'S SECRET

Don't waste time looking at how your friends are doing!

The decline of Henry's old companions is almost complete with Bardolph's execution for this most despicable petty theft. The King's ready support for the hanging shows how completely he has turned his back on the lowlife.

Montjoy, the French herald, arrives with a message from the King of France. King Charles wishes to know how much Henry is prepared to pay in ransom, though he doubts if the English can afford to raise a sum which would compensate for the damage they have done. He also maintains that Henry has betrayed his followers by leading them to their doom in France.

CHECKPOINT 14

Why does it make sense to treat the French people gently?

Henry compliments Montjoy on his conduct and bearing, 'Thou dost thy office fairly' (line 138), and sends a very honest reply to King Charles. He says that his army is weakened through sickness and he wishes to avoid a fight and return to Calais. However, he will fight if anyone stands in his way. After Montjoy leaves, Henry expresses the view that they are 'in God's hand' (line 168), and orders his men to make camp. Montjoy is one of the French characters who gains our respect. Henry admires his courage and dignity.

> ### Henry's leadership
>
> Henry shows some of his kingly qualities in this scene. He is firm in imposing discipline in his army, generous in his praise of good conduct, even in an enemy, honest in his dealings with King Charles, humble and pious in his trust in God and brave and defiant in the face of danger.
>
> Henry no longer appears to be the aggressor as he is trying to avoid a fight.

EXAMINER'S SECRET
You will not get high marks simply by retelling the story.

SCENE 7 – Before Agincourt in the French camp

❶ Again the French nobles are seen to be overconfident.

❷ Rambures is tempting fate.

❸ The French nobles are in boastful mood.

The French are waiting impatiently for morning and expect an easy victory over the English. The Dauphin, who has now joined the campaign, tries to outdo the others in praise of his horse and the conversation turns into an idle exchange of witticisms. He boasts that his 'way shall be paved with English faces' (line 81). One of the nobles, Rambures, suggests a game of dice for the ransoms of the prisoners they expect to capture. After the Dauphin leaves to put on his armour, the Constable expresses doubts about his bravery: 'I think he will eat all he kills' (line 92). The Constable's remarks about the Dauphin are quite witty but they are destructive and show he has no confidence in the royal prince.

There is no obvious leader among the French forces. The Dauphin, who is the most senior in rank, does not have the wholehearted support or respect of his nobles. The French are passing their time in idle boasting and gossip. This contrasts with the serious and practical approach of King Henry.

CHECK THE NET
Search for 'Agincourt' to learn more about the historical battle.

Scene 7 continued

CHECKPOINT 15

Why are the French so concerned about taking prisoners?

A messenger reports that the English are camped nearby. The Constable expresses pity for King Henry and both he and Orleans feel that it is sheer stupidity that keeps the English from running away. He calls them, 'fat-brained' (line 133) and 'Foolish curs' (line 142). Orleans anticipates a rich haul of prisoners. The French use images of animals when discussing the English soldiers which suggests they think of them as being less than human.

Now take a break!

Who says?

1 'Be copy now to men of grosser blood / And teach them how to war'

....

2 'I would give all my fame for a pot of ale and safety'

....

3 'for, look you, the mines is not according to the disciplines of the wars'

....

4 'Fortune is Bardolph's foe, and frowns on him, / For he hath stolen a pax, / And hanged must 'a be, a damned death!'

....

5 'We would not seek a battle as we are, / Nor as we are, we say, we will not shun it'

....

6 'Will it never be day? I will trot tomorrow a mile, and my way shall be paved with English faces'

....

About whom?

7 'he is white-livered and red-faced, by the means whereof 'a faces it out but fights not'

....

8 'And in a captive chariot into Rouen / Bring him our prisoner'

....

9 'Why, this is an arrant counterfeit rascal, I remember him now – a bawd, a cutpurse'

....

10 'I think he will eat all he kills'

....

Check your answers on page 75.

CHORUS – The night before the battle

❶ The Chorus describes the sights and sounds of the night before the battle.

The two armies are camped near each other and the Chorus contrasts the overconfident French with the war-weary English who seem like ghosts. We hear that Henry is visiting his soldiers and that his confident and friendly manner gives them comfort. Henry's relationship with his troops is seen as friendly, comforting and inspiring: 'A little touch of Harry in the night' (line 47). The name 'Harry' emphasises the King's friendly relationship with his men. His glance is like a ray of sunshine. The unequal nature of the coming contest is emphasised, as is the difference in attitude between the boastful French and the weary but patient English.

The Chorus again asks our pardon for presenting such great events with such limited resources, 'four or five most vile and ragged foils' (line 50). This description compensates for the limitations of the Shakespearean theatre.

DID YOU KNOW?

In Shakespeare's time, the plays were performed in daylight with few sound effects and little or no scenery.

SCENE 1 – Henry, the night before Agincourt

❶ Henry talks in a friendly fashion to some of his nobles.

❷ In disguise, he tests the mood of his ordinary soldiers.

❸ Finally, he asks for God's help.

This scene provides a slow and sombre prelude to the excitement and activity of the battle.

King Henry is discussing with the Duke of Gloucester the dangerous position they are in when they meet the Duke of Bedford and Sir Thomas Erpingham, an elderly knight. Henry talks cheerfully to them and borrows Sir Thomas's cloak. He sends them to tell the other lords to meet him in his tent. We see the friendly relationship between Henry and his nobles and his obvious affection for the elderly Sir Thomas as he wishes 'a good soft pillow for that good white head' (line 14).

There is no boasting among the English leaders.

When the others have left, Henry is challenged by Pistol. He does not reveal his identity and claims to be a Welshman. This causes Pistol to brag about what he intends to do to Fluellen – 'Tell him I'll knock his leek about his pate,' (line 55) – and when Henry claims to be Fluellen's kinsman, he insults him and leaves. Pistol and Fluellen provide a little humour to lighten this rather brooding and reflective scene. We can anticipate sparks when these two meet again.

Fluellen and Gower then enter. Gower greets Fluellen who tells him at great length to talk less because of the nearness of the enemy. There is simple comedy in Fluellen's long-winded explanation as to why Gower should keep quiet. Gower is the straight man in these scenes involving the captains. They leave without seeing Henry.

Three ordinary soldiers, Court, Bates and Williams, enter. Dawn is breaking and they view it with apprehension. When they see Henry he pretends to be a soldier under Sir Thomas Erpingham's command. They discuss the King and his responsibilities. Bates thinks the King would rather be 'in Thames up to the neck' (line 115) than here in France. Henry disagrees. Bates then says he would prefer that the King was on his own and could be ransomed without loss of life. Henry says that he would be happy to die with the King because his cause is just.

Bates and Williams say that they are there because they are the King's subjects and that this absolves them from any responsibility for whether the cause is just or not. The King will carry the responsibility if any of his men die in sin. Henry argues that each man is responsible to God for his own sins and the state of his soul and should therefore prepare himself before the battle so that he may die in a state of grace or live on as an example to others.

Williams expresses doubts about the King's intention to refuse personal ransom to save his life and he and Henry quarrel over this. They agree to settle their differences after the battle and exchange gloves which they will wear in their hats so as to recognise one another. Bates reminds them that they have 'French quarrels enough' (line 220) to deal with. We are given some insight into the

CHECKPOINT 16

Why does Henry approve of Fluellen?

EXAMINER'S SECRET

When writing about a specific scene or extract always make connections with the play as a whole – this at least shows you have read the complete work!

GLOSSARY

foils light fencing swords

views of the common soldiers and we are reminded that their deaths would leave their families destitute.

The burdens of power

Our respect for Henry is enhanced because we know he takes his responsibilities seriously and is not merely pursuing personal gain and honour.

He speaks to his soldiers man to man and does not take refuge in his rank and power, even when he is threatened with violence.

When the soldiers leave, Henry speaks his thoughts about the heavy burdens of kingship. He questions the value of ceremony and the trappings of royalty and contrasts the uneasy responsibilities of power with the simple, irresponsible life of the slave who can sleep peacefully each night.

DID YOU KNOW?

Henry is still worried that God may punish him because his father caused the death of King Richard II.

Sir Thomas Erpingham arrives to tell Henry that his nobles are looking for him. He says he will meet them at his tent. Alone again, Henry prays to God to give his soldiers courage: 'O God of battles, steel my soldiers' hearts; / Posses them not with fear' (lines 286–7). He asks God not to punish him on this particular day for the sins of his father. (Henry IV had deposed Richard II who was later murdered.) Henry says he has done his best to compensate for this.

He has wept, paid for prayers to be said and has built two chapels dedicated to Richard. He promises to do more. Henry is pious. He prays sincerely and has tried to make amends for his father's sins.

The Duke of Gloucester comes to take him to the meeting.

SCENE 2 – The French prepare for battle

❶ The French make jokes about the pathetic state of the English army.

It is morning and the French lords are preparing confidently for battle. A messenger informs them that the English army is in position. Henry is a competent general and has drawn up his forces before the French are ready. He has chosen the ground.

The Constable remarks that there are scarcely enough English to give them a decent battle: 'There is not work enough for all our hands' (line 18). He fears that the enemy will be so overwhelmed by their approach that they will surrender without a fight. We are again reminded of the great French advantage in numbers and the weakness of the English forces.

The Earl of Grandpré enters and calls upon the French nobles to hurry. He describes the English – 'Yon island carrions' (line 38) – as miserable and disgusting in their appearance. The Dauphin mockingly suggests that they feed and clothe the enemy before they fight them. Led by the Constable they head for the battlefield

Once again, the arrogance and contempt of the French lords help to increase the audience's anticipation of their defeat and humiliation.

SCENE 3 – Henry rallies his men for a final battle

❶ Henry inspires his troops.

❷ Once more he refuses to be ransomed.

The English leaders are assembled before the battle. We hear that King Henry has gone to view the enemy forces. His army is

EXAMINER'S SECRET
Higher-level achievement begins at the point when you show you are aware of being marked.

outnumbered by five to one. The Earl of Salisbury leaves to take up his position and bids a friendly farewell to the others.

EXAMINER'S SECRET

Plan your answers then you won't repeat yourself.

When the King returns, Westmorland says he wishes they had, 'ten thousand of those men in England / That do no work today!' (lines 17–18). Henry disagrees and points out, 'The fewer men, the greater share of honour' (line 22). Henry cleverly makes a virtue out their small numbers to inspire confidence in his followers.

> ### How to make mortals into heroes
>
> They are about to make history. Henry also flatters his men by calling them his brothers. To emphasise this point he offers free passage home for any man who wishes to leave. He tells them that this is the feast day of St Crispian and promises that those who survive will never forget it. On the anniversary they will be proud to show their wounds and tell the story of the battle. It will be passed down in history and 'gentlemen in England now abed / Shall think themselves accursed they were not here' (lines 64–5).

Salisbury arrives to announce that the French are ready to attack. He is followed by Montjoy the herald with another enquiry about Henry's ransom price should he be captured. Henry offers nothing but his bones, if the French can manage to kill him. He sends a defiant reply to the Constable of France saying that his soldiers may look poor and dirty – 'warriors for the working-day' (line 109) – but their hearts are ready and willing. He tells Montjoy not to come asking about ransom again.

Before they all leave for the battlefield, Henry generously grants the Duke of York the honour of commanding the vanguard.

SCENE 4 – On the battlefield

❶ Pistol takes a prisoner.

During the battle Pistol, whose exaggerated language and assumed courage and ferocity are ludicrous, captures a French soldier. They

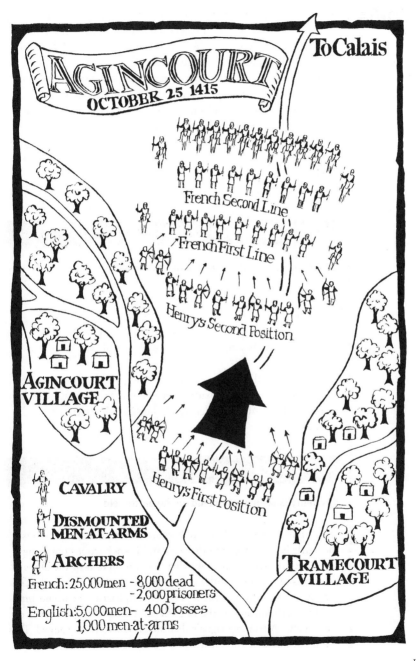

AGINCOURT
OCTOBER 25 1415

To Calais

French Second Line

French First Line

Henry's Second Position

AGINCOURT VILLAGE

CAVALRY

DISMOUNTED MEN-AT-ARMS

ARCHERS

Henry's First Position

TRAMECOURT VILLAGE

French: 25,000 men – 8,000 dead
– 2,000 prisoners
English: 5,000 men – 400 losses
1,000 men-at-arms

CHECKPOINT 17

On what other
occasion are
language problems
used for comic
effect?

are unable to understand each other. Pistol misinterprets the
Frenchman's words, and threatens him while demanding a ransom.
He thinks that 'moi' is a coin. This is a humorous interlude in the
battle, made comic by the language problem. The Boy acts as
interpreter and the prisoner promises to pay two hundred crowns.
Pistol leaves with his captive and the Boy comments on Pistol's
loud-mouthed cowardice: 'I never did know so full a voice issue
from so empty a heart' (lines 67–8). We hear that Nym has been
hanged as well as Bardolph. The Boy returns to the army's baggage
train which, he says, is vulnerable to French attack. These fears are
well founded as he will be killed in the process and we are reminded
of the serious nature of warfare.

SCENE 5 – French pride in defeat

1 The French realise they are losing the battle.

The Dauphin and the other French leaders witness with horror and
shame the defeat of their forces. They bitterly remember their
boasts and how confident they were of victory. The Dauphin's
suggestion that they should stab themselves is almost laughable.

In despair they throw themselves into the fight hoping to salvage
their honour by dying in battle. They do not try to organise their
forces – 'The devil take order now!' (line 22) – but charge for
reasons of damaged pride. This is a pointless act.

SCENE 6 – A ruthless act

1 Henry is seen in command on the battlefield.

King Henry enters with his soldiers and some prisoners. He says
the battle is going well but there are still French troops opposing
them. Exeter arrives with a moving description of how the Duke of
York was killed along with his close friend the Earl of Suffolk. This
account of the deaths of the two nobles emphasises the friendship
and brotherhood among the English and exemplifies self-sacrifice
and loyalty. A trumpet signals that the French have regrouped. This
creates dramatic tension just when we thought the battle was won.

> **Ruthlessness**
>
> We may feel that Henry's order that 'every soldier kill his prisoners!' (line 37) is the act of a man brutalised by his experience of battle.
>
> Henry, however, has very practical reasons for this. He has a small army and he does not want his soldiers to be hindered by their captives or distracted by thoughts of ransom.

SCENE 7 – The battle draws to a close

1 The French have killed the boys with the baggage.

2 The battle is coming to a close.

3 The French Herald asks permission to gather the dead.

Fluellen and Gower are outraged that some of the French have attacked the English baggage train and killed the boys. 'Kill the poys and the luggage! 'Tis expressly against the law of arms,' (lines 1–2) says Fluellen. They praise Henry's action in having the French prisoners killed. The French are shown in a bad light with their cowardly attack on the baggage train. It perhaps balances out against the killing of the French prisoners. Gower seems to think it is justified.

Fluellen is proud of Henry's Welsh connections – 'Ay, he was porn at Monmouth,' (line 11) – and compares him with Alexander the Great. Fluellen's pronunciation is confusing and comical.

Henry enters having beaten off the latest attack. The English have taken more prisoners including the Duke of Bourbon. He sees more French and sends a message to say that if they neither come and fight nor retreat then he will kill these prisoners and attack without mercy.

Montjoy arrives to ask permission for the French to retrieve their dead. He says to Henry, 'The day is yours' (line 85), and the King immediately praises God. Henry once again shows his modesty and piety when he credits God with the victory and prohibits boasting on pain of death.

? DID YOU KNOW?

Taking wealthy prisoners and selling them back for ransom was a major part of medieval warfare. Poor soldiers were not worth anything so were shown no mercy.

Fluellen reminds Henry of the good service of the Welsh soldiers in a previous war and Henry acknowledges Fluellen as a fellow countryman.

The King sees Williams, the soldier he had quarrelled with the previous night. Williams does not recognise Henry and says he is looking for the man who wears his glove as a token so that he can box his ears. Henry knows Fluellen has a fiery temper and, for a joke, sets up Fluellen with the glove but sends Warwick and Gloucester after him to see that no harm comes of it. The King shows his human side here.

SCENE 8 – The final tally

❶ Henry sees the end of his joke.

❷ He gives all credit to God for the victory.

CHECKPOINT 18

On what other occasion has Henry shown mercy to a common man for speaking his mind?

Fluellen, acting on Henry's information, denounces Williams as a traitor, but Henry intervenes before things take a serious turn. He gives Williams a glove full of gold in compensation. We may feel that it is unfair of Henry to play a trick on a humble soldier, as he has such power over him, but Williams speaks up for himself. He represents the honest, plain-spoken English yeoman.

Henry reads out a list of the French noblemen who have been taken prisoner and those who are dead. This reminds us of Act III, Scene 5, when the French King named those who were to attack the English.

He then reads out the English losses which are very small. Fluellen asks Henry's permission to speak about the numbers of those killed in the battle. This is important to Fluellen as a professional soldier and a student of military history. He does not wish to boast but he likes to be in a position to put people to rights about such facts. Henry thanks God, to whom he gives all credit – 'O God, thy arm was here' (line 107) – and forbids boasting. He gives orders for prayers to be sung before the army returns to England.

 Now take a break!

WHO SAYS?

1 'art thou officer, / Or art thou base, common and popular?'

....

2 'There is not work enough for all our hands'

....

3 'O that we had here / But one ten thousand of those men in England / That do no work today!'

....

4 'We would not die in that man's company / That fears his fellowship to die with us'

....

5 'O perdurable shame! Let's stab ourselves'

....

6 'Kill the poys and the luggage! 'Tis expressly against the law of arms'

....

7 'O give us leave, great King, / To view the field in safety and dispose / Of their dead bodies'

....

ABOUT WHOM?

8 'every wretch, pining and pale before, / Beholding him plucks comfort from his looks'

....

9 'I never did know so full a voice issue from so empty a heart'

....

10 'Lives he, good uncle? Thrice within this hour / I saw him down, thrice up again and fighting'

....

Check your answers on page 75.

CHORUS – Return to England

❶ Henry returns to England in triumph.

We are told that Henry returns to England by way of Calais and receives an enthusiastic welcome. We hear how 'London doth pour out her citizens' (line 24) to greet him.

The Chorus glosses over a period of some years, omitting a number of historical events which Shakespeare does not wish to include in the play.

The Holy Roman Emperor visits England to negotiate a peace and eventually Henry returns to France.

SCENE 1 – A last look at the common soldier

❶ Fluellen takes his revenge on Pistol.

Gower asks Fluellen why he is wearing his leek when St David's day is past. Fluellen replies that he does so to provoke Pistol who has insulted him. Pistol arrives 'swelling like a turkey-cock' (lines 14–15) and Fluellen beats him and forces him to eat the leek while the serious and responsible Gower denounces him as a 'counterfeit cowardly knave' (line 70).

CHECKPOINT 19

Where do you think Fluellen got the idea of wearing something in his cap to provoke a quarrel?

Last touches of humour

As the play draw to its end, we are given a final glimpse of Henry's former companions. Now they are seen as unthreatening amusing characters and we realise just how far Henry has developed from the wildness of his youth.

The amusement offers light relief before the play ends but also serves as a reminder that these people – and the temptations they offer – are still very much with us.

When the captains leave, Pistol declares he will return to England to live by pimping and stealing. He will tell people that the scars he received from Fluellen are war-wounds. The last link with Henry's wild youth, Pistol disappears into the criminal underworld of London.

Fluellen's language and Pistol's overblown **parody** of heroic verse provide much of the humour in their encounters.

> **CHECKPOINT 20**
>
> On what other occasion do we hear about showing off war-wounds?

SCENE 2 – The loose ends tied up

1 France has been devastated by the war.

2 Henry leaves his delegates to discuss the peace terms.

3 Katherine agrees to marry Henry.

4 The French agree to the peace terms and the marriage.

King Henry, accompanied by his nobles, is welcomed by the French King and his Queen. The Duke of Burgundy, acting as intermediary, describes how warfare has laid waste much of France. This reminds us of the real destruction and suffering caused by the war.

Henry says that the French must agree to his demands if they want peace. The French King says he will look at these terms once more and give his answer. King Charles is again seen to be slow to make up his mind. This contrasts with Henry's decisive and determined nature.

Henry delegates Exeter and other nobles to discuss the treaty. He is left with Princess Katherine and her maid.

Henry asks Katherine if she will have him as a husband. He claims to be nothing more than a simple soldier, a man of action and that he is unable to court her with fine words: 'I know no ways to mince it in love but directly to say "I love you."' (lines 127–8).

It is hard to believe Henry's claim to be poor with words when we have witnessed his skill when encouraging his army, but perhaps we should admire him for his modesty.

 DID YOU KNOW?
Although Henry shows affection for Katherine, 'political' marriages were common at this time.

Katherine speaks partly in French and partly in broken English. She agrees to marry him if her father wishes it. Henry assures her that he does and persuades her to allow him to kiss her.

When the others return there is some teasing from the Duke of Burgundy. The French have agreed to the English demands, including Henry's marriage to Katherine, and Henry is declared heir to the French throne. The French King and Queen express the hope that the marriage will bring unity and peace to the two countries.

All Henry's demands have been granted. The play ends with his complete success.

EPILOGUE – A happy ending?

The Chorus apologises for the humble efforts of the author and once again for the limitations of the small theatre in the presentation of such glorious events: 'In little room confining mighty men' (line 3). He tells the audience that Henry's gains were lost during the reign of his son, Henry VI. This glorious period of English history did not last and was followed by defeat abroad and civil war at home. Shakespeare is perhaps making a point about the importance of unity and stability.

Shakespeare's plays dealing with the reign of Henry VI were first performed about ten years before he wrote *Henry V* and they would be familiar to many playgoers.

WHO SAYS?

1 'Not for Cadwallader and all his goats'

....

5 'Then shall I swear to Kate, and you to me, / And may our oaths well kept and prosperous be!'

....

2 'My duty to you both, on equal love, / Great Kings of France and England'

....

4 'God, the best maker of all marriages, / Combine your hearts in one, your realms in one!'

....

3 'I speak to thee plain soldier. If thou canst love me for this, take me'

....

ABOUT WHOM?

6 'Why, here he comes, swelling like a turkey-cock'

....

8 'Take her, fair son, and from her blood raise up / Issue to me'

....

7 'You thought that because he could speak English in the native garb he could not therefore handle an English cudgel'

....

Check your answers on page 75.

PART THREE

COMMENTARY

CHECK THE BOOK

The Face of Battle, John Keegan (Pimlico), a study of several battles, contains some interesting material about Agincourt.

THEMES

PATRIOTISM

We are reminded several times in the play of previous English exploits in France. The Battle of Crécy, 1346, when the French were defeated by Edward III and his son, the Black Prince, is mentioned by the Archbishop of Canterbury in Act I, Scene 2, and by King Charles in Act II, Scene 4. The rhetoric of the Chorus in his descriptions of the army's preparations for the expedition (Act II), and Henry's speeches before Harfleur and Agincourt are calculated to rouse patriotic feelings in the audience.

There are a number of ways in which the English are shown to advantage and presented as being superior to their enemies. The unity and fellowship among the English is contrasted with the discord among the French. The French are shown as vain and incompetent, defeated by a small, sickly English army. At one point Henry boasts that one Englishman is worth three Frenchmen. Shakespeare shows the English as being civilised in their sparing of Harfleur, when in reality, the town was sacked. In the play we are presented with the view that God is on the side of the English.

KINGSHIP

As mentioned in the section on Henry in **Characters**, we are presented with the ideal of kingship in Henry V. Piety, humility, learning, courage, leadership, restraint and mercy are all demonstrated in this 'mirror of all Christian kings' (Act II, Chorus). Perhaps Shakespeare intended Henry to be a flattering parallel for Queen Elizabeth. He was certainly aware of the need for unity and stability in his own time and would promote those qualities which he thought would maintain the security of the state. Henry does not recklessly attack France. He secures England first by dealing with traitors at home and by making provision against a Scottish attack.

WARFARE

In the Chorus's description of the preparations for invasion, at the beginning of Act II, we are given some idea of the excitement generated by the prospects of the glory and honour to be won in battle. Before Agincourt Henry tells his troops that they will be respected and envied for the rest of their lives if they survive. Even if they die, their names will live for ever. However, in addition to the **rhetoric** and the glories of the English victory, we are given indications of the darker aspects of war.

We also see that it attracts criminals and parasites, like Pistol, Bardolph and Nym, who only go to steal. As Pistol says, 'Let us to France, like horse-leeches, my boys, To suck, to suck, the very blood to suck!' (II.3.53–4).

Henry's speech to the Governor of Harfleur (Act III, Scene 3), gives some indication of the horrors involved in the sack of a town.

The night before Agincourt, Williams talks about the hardships suffered by the families of poor soldiers. Their wives and children may be left to starve if they are killed. They have no choice but to obey the King and it is suggested that the King bears a heavy responsibility for waging war. After Agincourt, Exeter gives an account of the bloody deaths of Suffolk and York (Act IV, Scene 6) and Burgundy, in Act V, Scene 2, describes the devastation caused by the war in France and regrets the abandonment of the peaceful pursuits of the arts and learning.

? DID YOU KNOW?

Some First World War poets wrote positive and patriotic poems, especially at the beginning of the war. In particular, look at 'For the Fallen' by Laurence Binyon and 'The Soldier' by Rupert Brooke. There are echoes of some of Henry's speeches in both. Compare the latter with Henry's speech to Montjoy in Act IV, Scene 3, where he says that the bodies of the English soldiers will continue to fight by rotting in the ground and causing a plague in France.

These negative views of war add depth and credibility to the drama but do not significantly detract from its main thrust which is towards a patriotic celebration of the English triumph.

LOVE AND FRIENDSHIP

One of the merits of the English side is the friendship between the leaders. Henry has affectionate words for Sir Thomas Erpingham and refers to him as 'old heart' (IV.1.34). Bedford and Exeter bid Salisbury a fond farewell before Agincourt, and we hear how, in the battle, the Duke of York kissed his dead friend Suffolk and died alongside him.

Henry extends his friendship to include all his soldiers and there is a general feeling of good fellowship in the English army.

The love between Henry and Katherine is not altogether convincing. Henry does tell Katherine he loves her, but he is clearly not about to die of it. Katherine agrees to marry him, but in reality she does not have much choice. Even though both Henry and Katherine try to make a good impression on the other, nothing can hide the fact that theirs is, first and foremost, a political union.

STRUCTURE

The structure and the unity of the play depend very much on the character of Henry as we see him exemplify the qualities of the ideal King. There are a number of events on the way to the achievement of his goals which do not, in themselves, form a strong plot.

These are:

- Discussion and justification of the war

- Preparation and the suppression of treason

- Campaigning and setback in France

- Victory at Agincourt

- A satisfactory treaty and marriage agreement

However, Shakespeare manages to create a drama around these events using the device of the Chorus who highlights their significance by:

- Filling in historical information, sometimes covering a span of several years

- Anticipating events so that the audience may have some knowledge not shared by characters, e.g. the exposure of the traitors

- Focusing our attention on the merits of Henry – 'This star of England' (Epilogue, line 6) – and emphasising his central role in these great events

The comic sub-plots involving the lowlife characters and Fluellen give the play some texture and light relief. The dishonesty and cowardice of some of these characters highlight the honesty and courage of Henry and his true followers. The lowlife characters help to link this play with the others in the group and maintain a sense of historical continuity.

The death of Falstaff can be seen as a signal that the days of Henry's youthful follies are truly dead and buried.

We are given regular views of the disunity and frivolity of the French leaders to emphasise the strength and harmony among the English:

- King Charles's hesitation and fear contrast with Henry's determination and decisive action.

- Henry's sensible desire to avoid battle when he is in a weak position (Act III, Scene 6) is contrasted with the Dauphin's foolish, posturing threat to stab himself in defeat.

- The friendship between Henry's nobles is set against the bickering and gossip of their French counterparts.

- Henry's piety is contrasted with the frivolity of the French, their tempting of fate in their boasts and their casual use of oaths.

EXAMINER'S SECRET
In a typical examination you might use as many as eight quotations.

Strong
Brave
Pious
Persuasive
Plain-spoken
Charismatic

 CHECK THE NET

Search for 'Henry V' to learn about the 'real' King.

CHARACTERS

KING HENRY

Henry dominates the play and completely overshadows the other characters. His words comprise about a third of the text.

Taken at face value it seems that Shakespeare has presented us with his view of the ideal monarch: 'the mirror of all Christian kings' (Act II, Chorus, line 6).

Henry is a devoutly religious man. We hear from the clergy that he is 'a true lover of the holy Church' (I.1.23) and that he is has a good knowledge of scripture and other areas of learning. He seeks the approval and support of the Church before waging war, and is aware of the horror and destruction which it brings. Henry prays sincerely, entrusting his enterprise to God's will and refusing to take credit for the victory at Agincourt, threatening with death any who boast of it and thus detract from God's achievement. He has paid for prayers and the building of chapels to compensate for his father's sins and after the battle he orders the singing of prayers and psalms in thanks to God. Unlike the French leaders, he does not use idle oaths or take God's name in vain.

Henry's physical courage is never in doubt. We see him leading his men at the siege of Harfleur and hear that he has been in personal combat at Agincourt.

As a leader of men Henry has wonderful insight. He encourages his nobles with references to their forefathers' deeds and flatters his men that he sees noble qualities in them. He reinforces their loyalty with talk of brotherhood and friendship and he leads by example. He refuses to arrange a ransom for himself. The Chorus tells us that the night before Agincourt he went around the English camp, inspiring his soldiers with confidence by his friendly words and cheerful manner. We can see that he takes his responsibilities seriously when he talks to Williams and the other common soldiers and later, in his only **soliloquy**, in which he talks of the heavy burden of kingship.

He is a skilful military commander and avoids useless loss of life. At Harfleur his eloquent warning to the Governor persuades him to surrender the town.

In matters of state Henry is firm and decisive. His reply to the Dauphin's 'tennis balls' insult is angry but dignified and restrained. He listens to the advice of others and considers such practical issues as the danger of a Scottish attack. He demands prompt replies from the French and will not be diverted from his goal. We see evidence of this on several occasions.

He dispenses justice in a fair and impartial manner. The three traitors are condemned because they have threatened the safety of the kingdom. He does not seek personal revenge and he can be magnanimous, as when he orders the release of the drunk who has shouted insults about him.

EXAMINER'S SECRET
A sign of a good candidate is the ability to cross-reference, e.g. provide evidence of Henry's sense of duty from different parts of the play.

Henry has qualities which encourage us to believe in him as a human being, not just a paragon of kingly virtues. He has a sense of humour as demonstrated in the trick he plays on Fluellen and Williams. He is awkward and blunt when speaking to Katherine and is unable to court her with conventional flowery phrases and compliments. In his soliloquy in Act IV, Scene 1, he reveals his feelings about the responsibilities of kingship and the emptiness of ceremony and adulation.

It is possible to take a more negative view of Henry and some critics have described him as a cynical, ruthless manipulator. His piety can be viewed as a front which masks his ambition. It could be argued that he is merely setting up potential scapegoats, or seeking to spread the blame should he fail, when he enlists the support of the Church.

We may think him cold-hearted as he has turned his back on his old drinking companions. We hear complaints that he has broken Falstaff's heart and he is unmoved by the report of Bardolph's execution. If we look back to *Henry IV, Part 1*, the young Prince Hal made it clear that he was using Falstaff and his companions and would cast them off when the time came to show himself in a better light (*Henry IV, Part 1*, Act I, Scene 2).

However there is no real evidence to support the view that King Henry is wilfully deceiving people about his motives and his piety. He is as sincere when speaking in **soliloquy** as he is in public, and it is accepted that Shakespeare's characters reveal their true thoughts when speaking alone. Finally, the Chorus, who we may think of as expressing the views of the author, is always positive about Henry and full of praise for 'This star of England' (Epilogue, line 6).

PISTOL

One of the old lowlife companions of Henry's youth, Pistol goes to France to profit from the war by thieving. He is a braggart and a coward who receives his just deserts at the hands of Fluellen. He speaks in a bombastic and ridiculous **parody** of **epic** verse full of **alliteration** and windy nonsense. He provides much of the humour in the play through his speech, his cowardly behaviour and his encounters with Fluellen. However our sympathy towards him is limited by his attempts to lead the Boy into a life of crime and by his determination to continue in his dishonesty and to lie about his war exploits.

BARDOLPH

Bardolph, another of the lowlife companions, is notable for his red nose, apparently the result of drinking. He is hanged for stealing from a church which causes a dispute between Pistol and Fluellen.

NYM

Nym is the third member of this gang. We first see him in a comic episode when he and Pistol threaten to fight each other, but both are too cowardly to do any harm. He does not say much but has a few catch-phrases such as, 'that's the humour of it' (for example, II.3.58). He, too, is hanged for stealing.

EXAMINER'S SECRET

It is always a good idea to collect a range of words to describe a character.

THE BOY

The Boy is an unwilling party to the thieves' schemes. He goes to France as their servant after his master, Falstaff, dies. He gives us sharp and perceptive descriptions of these rogues and he plans to leave their company as soon as possible. He does not wish to follow them in a life of crime. The fact that they have attempted to corrupt this youth affects the audience's attitude to them. Sadly, we must assume that the Boy is killed when the French attack the baggage train in Act IV.

FLUELLEN

The Welsh captain is a serious-minded professional soldier. His version of the English language provides some simple humour. He tends to pronounce 'b' as 'p' and this produces some comic effects such as when he speaks of 'Alexander the pig' (IV.7.13–14), when he means Alexander the big, or great. He is also comical when he tries to hold discussions on the theory of warfare in the midst of battle, referring to the classical authors. His peculiar English, combined with his use of learned expressions result in some very amusing passages.

He is a brave soldier and despises cowards like Pistol. He is hot-headed and quick to take offence. He is particularly proud of his nationality and takes great delight in King Henry's acknowledgement of his own Welsh connections. He makes Pistol eat a leek for insulting the Welsh emblem on St David's day.

Professional
Serious
Conscientious
Talkative
Loyal
Proud

GOWER

The English captain is an honest even-tempered soldier. He seems to have the respect of the other captains and acts as a straight man to Fluellen in a number of comic situations. He tries to keep the peace between Fluellen and Macmorris, he recognises Pistol as a rogue when Fluellen has been fooled by the coward's boasts at the bridge, and he approves of Fluellen's punishment of him in Act V, Scene 1.

MACMORRIS AND JAMY

These two captains appear only in Act II, Scene 2. Macmorris, the Irish captain, is quick-tempered and proud. He is a great believer in mines and gunpowder and he quarrels with Fluellen.

Jamy, the Scottish captain, is thoughtful and seems willing to discuss theory with Fluellen. Both captains speak in a comic version of their regional dialects.

The inclusion of English, Irish, Scots and Welsh captains may suggest that the whole of Britain is united against the French or that the English King has a right to rule over these countries. In fact,

England and Scotland were not united until 1603 when King James came to the throne. He was already King James VI of Scotland, and became King James I of England.

THE ENGLISH SOLDIERS

Bates, Court and Williams are three common soldiers who Henry visits in disguise the night before Agincourt. They are thoughtful, plain-spoken men. They know they have most to lose in battle as they are too poor to be worth capturing for ransom and if they are killed, their families will be destitute. Williams is the most outspoken of the three and eventually quarrels with Henry. After the battle when Henry reveals his identity, Williams still speaks up for himself and excuses himself in a dignified way. We do not see any French noble speaking to a common soldier and we hear references to mercenary troops in their army.

THE TRAITORS

Cambridge, Scroop and Grey all express remorse and accept their punishment when they are exposed. This is not a particularly convincing episode. It seems that they are so dazzled by Henry's perfection that they are glad to be caught. We are told that Scroop's treachery is particularly wicked because he had been a close and trusted companion of the King.

EXETER

The Duke of Exeter, Henry's uncle, is a staunch and loyal supporter of the young King. He arrests the traitors in Act II, Scene 2, and he delivers the King's demands to the French court in a very bold and forthright way in Act II, Scene 4. Henry regards him as being utterly reliable and leaves him in charge of Harfleur (Act III, Scene 3), after it has been captured. We hear of his bravery at the bridge from Fluellen in Act III, Scene 6. He is foremost among those who Henry delegates to settle the treaty in Act V, Scene 2, while he courts Katherine.

THE CHURCHMEN

The Archbishop of Canterbury and the Bishop of Ely are two schemers who are concerned with protecting the property and assets of the Church. It seems that they are happy to encourage

Henry to invade France and will even finance the venture as it will keep him from introducing the proposed heavy taxation of Church property. They go beyond their remit of providing legal advice when they actively encourage Henry to attack France with reminders of previous English victories.

KING CHARLES OF FRANCE

The French King is cautious and indecisive. He asks for time to consider Henry's demands in Act II, Scene 4, and again in Act V, Scene 2. He does not seem at all confident in the face of the English threat and refers to previous French defeats at the hands of Edward III. He eventually gives in to all of Henry's demands.

Weak
Indecisive
Cautious
Fearful

PRINCESS KATHERINE

Katherine is a lively, intelligent girl. She would have been fourteen at the time of Agincourt and eighteen when she became engaged to Henry. We see her sense of fun when she is attempting to learn English in Act III, Scene 4. She provides light relief in this scene between the serious events of the war. In the final scene she shows that she is loyal to her country when she questions whether she could love the enemy of France. She is an obedient daughter as she gives her consent to marry Henry only if her father wishes it.

THE DAUPHIN

The Dauphin is vain and overconfident. He dismisses Henry as a mere playboy and sends him the insult of the tennis balls. He boasts about his horse and about what he will do in the battle. However, he is almost comical when he suggests stabbing himself when the French are losing the fight. We are unsure about his position as a leader. At first King Charles does not allow him to go with the army, and he does not enjoy the confidence of the other French leaders, particularly the Constable of France.

THE CONSTABLE OF FRANCE

The Constable of France is a voice of reason among the French. He cautions them against dismissing Henry as an idle youth. He expresses a poor opinion of the Dauphin's courage before the battle and admits to a grudging sympathy for Henry: 'Alas, poor Harry of England! He longs not for the dawning as we do' (III.7.130–1).

MONTJOY, THE HERALD

Henry respects Montjoy for his courage and for the dignified and loyal way he carries out his duties, whether he is delivering a message of defiance from the French King or asking permission to gather the bodies of the dead after the defeat.

LANGUAGE AND STYLE

Two main types of speech are used in the play:

- Blank verse
- Prose

The noble and upper-class characters speak in **blank verse**, but occasionally may speak in **prose** if the subject matter is not important or if they are speaking to low-class characters. Blank verse elevates or raises the level of the language and is associated with nobility and noble ideas.

The French leaders speak in prose in Act II, Scene 7, as they are idly boasting and gossiping. They often use irreligious oaths and make indecent jokes. They make foul comparisons when speaking about the English: 'carrion' (IV.2.38), meaning dead meat.

King Henry speaks in prose when he is in disguise and talking to the soldiers as he is presenting himself as an ordinary man. He also uses prose when he is talking to Katherine, but this is to emphasise that he is a plain-spoken soldier and lacks fancy words with which to court her. Speaking in blank verse and elevated language would have made Henry seem like a proud conqueror rather than a suitor, especially when the princess has little English.

The verse is usually in lines of ten syllables. These are called **iambic pentameters** and are based on a pattern of five pairs of syllables, each pair consisting of an unstressed followed by a stressed syllable. An example of this verse is:

EXAMINER'S SECRET
A feature of A-grade writing on literature is the ability to see two possibilities of interpretations and to support a preference for one of them.

'For he today that sheds his blood with me
Shall be my brother; be he ne'er so vile,'

(IV.3.61–2)

This is the basic pattern but Shakespeare does not stick rigidly to this as it would become obvious and monotonous. Occasionally he uses a pair of **rhyming lines**, known as a rhyming couplet. This feature is often used to signal the end of a scene.

Prose is what we would consider everyday speech. This can vary a great deal. When Henry, in disguise, is speaking to the soldiers, he speaks in prose but it is rich and well-structured.

Fluellen speaks in a comic version of Welsh-English, using stock phrases like 'look you' (for example, III.2.100). His speech is further affected by his choice of vocabulary and his wish to discuss military theory.

Macmorris and Davy also speak in comic versions of their dialects.

Among the lower-class characters, Pistol is the only one who speaks in verse, but it is a parody, or **mock-heroic** type of verse. It is part of his boastful, bombastic pretence at bravery and is full of **alliteration** and ridiculous theatrical phrases, for example:

'O braggart vile and damned furious wight
The grave doth gape, and doting death is near;'

(II.1.61–2)

In speeches like this Shakespeare was probably making fun of the style used by some other playwrights.

In the Chorus and in some of Henry's speeches there are elements of **rhetoric**, repetition of words or phrases, the building up of lists or questions and the balancing of phrases, for example:

'We few, we happy few, we band of brothers.'

(IV.3.60)

EXAMINER'S SECRET

An A-grade student is able to provide a detailed account of language features, or structured patterns, to support a conclusion about the author's intentions

'...Show men dutiful?
Why, so didst thou. Seem they grave and learned?
Why, so didst thou. Came they of noble family?
Why, so didst thou. Seem they religious?
Why, so didst thou.'

(II.2.127–31)

'Like little body with a mighty heart,'

(II.0.17)

The play contains several long speeches. This is to be expected in such a patriotic and rousing story where the audience are treated to complex and persuasive arguments.

In Act I the church leaders give the audience necessary background information. The country has gone through a period of crisis, a 'scambling and unquiet time' (I.1.4). The church is threatened with severe taxation and the bishops are looking for a way out. We hear about Henry's reformed character and his proposed war on France. All of this prepares the audience for the first scene with Henry and gives the audience an insider's view of the bishops' advice to the King.

EXAMINER'S SECRET
A candidate who is capable of arriving at unusual, well-supported judgements *independently* is likely to receive the highest marks.

The language in this first scene is elevated and full of fine images, particularly when referring to Henry and his transformation from a dissolute youth. His present body is described as 'a paradise / T'envelop and contain celestial spirits' (I.1.30–1) and his conversation is full of 'sweet and honeyed sentences' (I.1.50).

A number of recurring **images** and words are used in the play. We find words to do with speedy movement and flying, for example 'our wings' (I.2.00), 'winged heels, as English Mercuries' (II.0.7), 'winged thoughts' (V.0.8).

These images suggest the freedom and speed of birds, the superhuman qualities of Mercury, the messenger of the gods and the holy attributes of angels.

The fierceness of the English soldiers is suggested by comparisons with wild animals, 'they will eat like wolves and fight like devils' (III.7.149–50), and hunting dogs, 'I see you stand like greyhounds in the slips, / Straining upon the start' (III.1.31–2). At Harfleur, Henry encourages them to 'imitate the action of the tiger' (III.1.6).

When Henry uses these animal images, although they suggest violence and ferocity, they are positive and complimentary, for example, greyhounds are well-bred hunting dogs. The Duke of Orleans, however, contemptuously calls the English, 'Foolish curs' (III.7.142). Even when the French acknowledge English bravery, it is connected with stupidity rather than nobility.

EXAMINER'S SECRET

Avoid topics that have nothing directly to do with the question.

Violence is also suggested by images of storms and other violent natural events such as whirlpools and earthquakes, for example,

> '... his approaches makes as fierce
> As waters to the sucking of a gulf'
>
> (II.4.9–10)

> 'Therefore in fierce Tempest is he coming,
> In thunder and in earthquake, like a Jove,'
>
> (II.4.99–100)

and

> '... let the brow o'erwhelm it
> As fearfully as doth a galled rock
> O'erhang and jutty his confounded base,
> Swilled with the wild and wasteful ocean.'
>
> (III.1.11–14)

The images of wild nature and fierce animals, which occur throughout the play, help to create an atmosphere of violence and danger.

Now take a break!

GLOSSARY

Foolish curs low-born mongrels

PART FOUR

RESOURCES

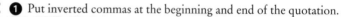

HOW TO USE QUOTATIONS

One of the secrets of success in writing essays is the way you use quotations. There are five basic principles:

1 Put inverted commas at the beginning and end of the quotation.

2 Write the quotation exactly as it appears in the original.

3 Do not use a quotation that repeats what you have just written.

4 Use the quotation so that it fits into your sentence.

5 Keep the quotation as short as possible.

EXAMINER'S SECRET

Short, snappy quotations are always the best.

When you use quotations in this way, you are demonstrating the ability to use text as evidence to support your ideas - not simply including words from the original to prove you have read it.

Your comment should not duplicate what is in your quotation. For example:

> **Fluellen refuses to intercede on behalf of Bardolph, and would be happy to see his own brother hanged in such circumstances because he believes in discipline: 'for if, look you, he were my brother, I would desire the Duke to use his good pleasure and put him to execution; for discipline ought to be used'.**
>
> (III.6.53–5).

EXAMINER'S SECRET

There is no need to always provide lengthy quotations. Key words like 'mettle' (III.5.15) taken from the text can be more effective.

Far more effective is to write:

> **Fluellen says he will not help Bardolph. If he were his own brother he would, 'desire the Duke to use his good pleasure and put him to execution; for discipline ought to be used'.**
>
> (III.6.54–5).

However, the most sophisticated way of using the writer's words is to embed them into your sentence:

Fluellen says that if Bardolph were his own brother he would wish the Duke to, 'put him to execution', because he believes, 'discipline ought to be used'

(III.6.54–5).

COURSEWORK ESSAY

Set aside an hour or so at the start of your work to plan what you have to do.

- List all the points you feel are needed to cover the task. Collect page references of information and quotations that will support what you have to say. A helpful tool is the highlighter pen: this saves painstaking copying and enables you to target precisely what you want to use.

- Focus on what you consider to be the main points of the essay. Try to sum up your argument in a single sentence, which could be the closing sentence of your essay. Depending on the essay title, it could be a ...statement about a character: Just as Henry represents the ideal of kingship, Williams is the ideal of the ordinary plain-spoken Englishman; an opinion about setting: The French court is a place of weakness, indecision and disunity; or a judgement on a theme: The play, Henry V, is a treatise on the qualities of the ideal monarch.

- Make a short essay plan. Use the first paragraph to introduce the argument you wish to make. In the following paragraphs develop this argument with details, examples and other possible points of view. Sum up your argument in the last paragraph. Check you have answered the question.

- Write the essay, remembering all the time the central point you are making.

- On completion, go back over what you have written to eliminate careless errors and improve expression. Read it aloud to yourself, or, if you are feeling more confident, to a relative or friend.

If you can, try to type your essay, using a word processor. This will allow you to correct and improve your writing without spoiling its appearance.

EXAMINER'S SECRET
Always read the whole examination paper before you start writing.

SITTING THE EXAMINATION

Examination papers are carefully designed to give you the opportunity to do your best. Follow these handy hints for exam success:

BEFORE YOU START

- Make sure you know the subject of the examination so that you are properly prepared and equipped.

- You need to be comfortable and free from distractions. Inform the invigilator if anything is off-putting, e.g. a shaky desk.

- Read the instructions, or rubric, on the front of the examination paper. You should know by now what you have to do but check to reassure yourself.

- Observe the time allocation – and follow it carefully. If they recommend 60 minutes for Question 1 and 30 minutes for Question 2, it is because Question 1 carries twice as many marks.

- Consider the mark allocation. You should write a longer response for 4 marks than for 2 marks.

WRITING YOUR RESPONSES

- Use the questions to structure your response, e.g. question: 'The endings of X's poems are always particularly significant. Explain their importance with reference to two poems.' The first part of your answer will describe the ending of the first poem; the second part will look at the ending of the second poem; the third part will be an explanation of the significance of the two endings.

- Write a brief draft outline of your response.

- A typical 30-minute examination essay is probably between 400 and 600 words in length.

- Keep your writing legible and easy to read, using paragraphs to show the structure of your answers.

- Spend a couple of minutes afterwards quickly checking for obvious errors.

EXAMINER'S SECRET

As you write, check that you are still answering the question. It is surprisingly easy to start well and drift off the subject entirely.

WHEN YOU HAVE FINISHED

- Don't be downhearted – if you found the examination difficult, it is probably because you really worked at the questions. Let's face it, they are not meant to be easy!

- Don't pay too much attention to what your friends have to say about the paper. Everyone's experience is different and no two people ever give the same answers.

EXAMINER'S SECRET
Always check your answer when you have finished.

IMPROVE YOUR GRADE

As a student of English Literature you will be assessed on your ability to respond to the play in detail and with sensitivity. The examiner will expect you to show that you know and appreciate the contents of the play. You should be able to select and include relevant material that supports your views and comments.

The examiner will also want to see that you appreciate Shakespeare's use of language and how it contributes to the play. You should also show that you are aware of the social context and historical background. This refers to the time when the play was written and not the time of the actions depicted in the play.

Do not forget that the play was written to be performed. Try to imagine the performance in your head when reading the text. If you read with performance in mind you are more likely to appreciate Shakespeare's intentions and skills.

EXAMINER'S SECRET
If you are asked to make a comparison, use comparing words such as 'on the other hand', 'however' and 'by contrast'.

PLOT AND STRUCTURE

It is important to have an overall view of the story and the way it is built or structured. This is fairly well marked out for you in *Henry V* in the five acts:

- In Act I we get to know Henry and his intentions.

- In Act II we anticipate the invasion and get a glimpse of the opposition.

- In Act III we are shown initial success followed by danger.

- In Act IV we have a glorious victory against superior odds.

- In Act V we are shown Henry as human and gentle, but in control.

The sub-plots involve the lowlife characters and Fluellen. These provide light relief.

CHARACTERS

Henry is the hero and main character of our play. He does not change much in the play but we hear how he has changed from what he was in the past. He does have several different aspects. The strong and decisive leader, the brave warrior, the skilful and cautious politician, the religious and humble man, the warm friend and the joker. You should be able to point to evidence of these aspects if you mention them. The evidence does not always lie in Henry's own words and actions. We often learn from the reports of others, for example in Act I, Scene1.

This is also the case when discussing the qualities of any of the other characters in the play.

EXAMINER'S SECRET

Support your opinions. Give reasons.

Obviously we judge characters by the way they behave in the play and the way they relate to others and deal with situations. We may not all have the same feelings towards particular characters. If that was the case then the examiner's job would be very tedious. Our responses may be determined by our age, sex, ethnic origin, social class or occupation. We often identify with characters in a play: we put ourselves in their shoes. We may be surprised to find that others may not identify with the same characters as we do. If you express personal opinions or preferences, be prepared to back them up.

THEMES AND IDEAS

There are a number of moral issues and ideas dealt with in *Henry V*. It is important to identify these and to decide where you stand in relation to them. Is Henry glorifying war when he encourages his men to fight? There are several occasions when we are told about the horrific effects of war. What are we to think about this? Where does Shakespeare stand? There are no easy answers to this sort of question. If you have an answer, then support it.

LANGUAGE

When dealing with language be ready to explain what is meant, to explain and explore the effects of the language and to relate it to the character and the situation.

Henry's description of his men as 'greyhounds in the slips' (III.1.31) is an appropriate and effective image for a number of reasons. It is a hunting image. Hunting is a sport of kings and nobles and these soldiers are under his control and are about to be let loose on the enemy like a pack of dogs. It is an animalistic and brutal image which is appropriate to the battle situation, and it suggests that the enemy is a vulnerable prey which will inevitably fall to the hunters. Greyhounds are sleek and thin dogs and at this time Henry's army are weary and undernourished so it may also suggest their physical appearance.

EXAMINER'S SECRET

An A-grade candidate can analyse a variety of the writer's techniques.

HUMOUR

How do we explain why something is funny?

Pistol is a vain cowardly character who tries to get his way by blustering and boasting.

When he calls Nym a 'braggart vile' (II.1.61) it is funny because Pistol is the greatest braggart or boaster in the play.

EXAMINER'S SECRET

Everything you write on your answer sheet is marked.

The character of Fluellen provides humour, partly through his character and his actions but to a great extent through the way he speaks. Shakespeare raises a laugh out of his Welsh version of English. 'What do you call the town where Alexander the pig was born?' (IV.7.12). He means 'big' or 'great' and he pronounces his *b*s as *p*s. This is quite low-level humour but is still quite popular today. The audience laugh at his incompetence with the English language.

PLANNING

Always plan your answers, whatever method you use. Some people like to make lists or bullet points, others use spidergraphs but keep an eye on the time.

Think carefully about the question and underline key words in it. If the question asks you to compare, it is essential that you do so. Separate pieces on characters and events with no comparison will result in poor marks for this type of question.

EXAMINER'S SECRET

If you have been asked to compare and do not do so you will not achieve a good grade.

Identify passages which will be important in answering the question. This will help when you begin to write your answer.

Keep thinking about the text when you are working on your answer. Support your opinions by referring to the play. Some candidates get carried away by wondering what might have happened if someone had done something different. You can get lost down this road.

Remember that the examiner has read the book. You will not get much credit for merely telling the story. Refer to events if you are making a point about them.

Consider why people do things and why they say things. What are their motives? What effect do they have? How do they relate to the main themes and ideas of the play?

SAMPLE ESSAY PLAN

A typical essay question on Henry V is followed by a sample essay plan in note form. This does not present the only answer to the question, merely one answer. Do not be afraid to include your own ideas and leave out some of those in the sample. Remember that quotations or close references to the text are essential to prove and illustrate the points you make.

How does Shakespeare seek to make us respond to Henry as a man?

Look through the play for occasions when Henry displays what you would consider to be human qualities as opposed to purely kingly virtues.

PART 1

Refer to the question. We have many examples of his kingly qualities. Name them. Perhaps give brief examples.

PART 2

Describe occasions where Henry shows affection and generosity, for example:

EXAMINER'S SECRET

You are always given credit for writing your essay plans.

EXAMINER'S SECRET

If the rubric gives planning time, **use it** to plan your answers!

- Release of the drunkard who insulted him
- Towards Sir Thomas Erpingham
- Friendly greetings to other nobles
- His generosity towards Montjoy
- His generosity towards the Duke of York

PART 3

Describe Henry's relationships with the lower-class characters, for example:

- His approval of and relationship with Fluellen
- His talk with Williams and the others

PART 4

Discuss Henry's soliloquy where he thinks about the burden of his responsibilities.

PART 5

Consider Henry's sense of humour, the joke he plays on Fluellen and Williams. Perhaps this is cruel or merely some light relief after the strain he has been under.

PART 6

Modesty and openness, for example he:

- Is quite frank about his weak position when speaking to Montjoy
- Allows the Duke of York to take the most honoured command in the battle
- Makes no attempt at courtliness with Katherine

CONCLUSION

Consider the above qualities and examples and consider how far they show Henry to be a sympathetic and credible human being.

EXAMINER'S SECRET

Any marks gained by a lot of extra time spent on one question is unlikely to make up for marks lost on another.

FURTHER QUESTIONS

Make a plan as shown above and attempt these questions.

1 To what extent is Henry, 'the mirror of all Christian kings'?

2 What are the functions of the Chorus and how effective is he?

3 Discuss the ways in which Henry inspires his men before Harfleur and before Agincourt.

4 Compare and contrast the French court and nobles with the English.

5 Shakespeare creates humour through characters, situations and language. Discuss this with reference to one humorous scene.

6 How does Shakespeare create the impression of large-scale battles on his small stage?

7 Does Henry V present a narrow and nationalistic view of history that has little to offer today's audience?

8 Are Henry's religious devotion and piety convincing?

9 Does the glorification of war overshadow the reminders of its horrors in the play?

10 Is Fluellen a figure of fun, a hero, or both?

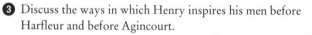

EXAMINER'S SECRET

Always have a spare pen!

Now take a break!

alliteration a series of similar consonant sounds, usually at the beginnings of words, to give rhythm or emphasis to a passage

blank verse lines which have a rhythmical pattern but do not rhyme. Most of this play is in blank verse, with iambic pentameters as the type of verse used

epic a long narrative poem dealing with a great hero, or a work or story on a similar theme

iambic pentameter a line of verse with five pairs of syllables, each pair consisting of an unstressed and a stressed syllable

image/imagery a picture in words either comparing one thing with another or giving it the qualities of another

mock-heroic treating a trivial subject with ridiculous, comic grandeur. Most of Pistol's speech is mock-heroic

parody an imitation which ridicules the original

patronage support of an artist by a wealthy person

prose ordinary spoken or written language, without set pattern or regular rhythm

pun a play on words; using a word that has two very different meanings. The Elizabethans were fond of puns and considered that someone who could pun well was intelligent

rhetoric the art of persuasive speaking. During the Middle Ages it was an essential subject of study

soliloquy a speech made by a character directly to the audience which reveals his or her thoughts

CHECKPOINT 1 Because Shakespeare's theatre was a circular wooden construction.

CHECKPOINT 2 England and France.

CHECKPOINT 3 It will divert Henry's attention from taxing the church.

CHECKPOINT 4 The Scots may invade England.

CHECKPOINT 5 The churchmen have told us that he is a reformed character (Act I, Scene 1).

CHECKPOINT 6 A Scottish invasion.

CHECKPOINT 7 The English are united under a strong leader. The French argue and have a weak King.

CHECKPOINT 8 The French King hesitates when faced with such an important challenger.

CHECKPOINT 9 Gower – English, Fluellen – Welsh, Jamy – Scottish, Macmorris – Irish.

CHECKPOINT 10 He was ambassador to the French King.

CHECKPOINT 11 The French have offered her in marriage to Henry.

CHECKPOINT 12 They are beaten by those people that they hold in much contempt.

CHECKPOINT 13 Pistol, Nym and the boy.

CHECKPOINT 14 They are more likely to co-operate if they are treated well and Henry wishes to become their King.

CHECKPOINT 15 Because they hope to gain ransoms for them.

CHECKPOINT 16 He is a loyal and conscientious soldier.

CHECKPOINT 17 When Princess Katherine is learning English in Act III, Scene 4.

CHECKPOINT 18 The drunk in Southampton (Act II, Scene 2, line 40).

CHECKPOINT 19 Williams and the glove in Act III, Scenes 7 and 8.

CHECKPOINT 20 When Henry inspires his men before Agincourt.

TEST YOURSELF (ACT I)

1 Archbishop of Canterbury (*Scene 1*)

2 King Henry (*Scene 2*)

3 Bishop of Ely (*Scene 2*)

4 French Ambassador (*Scene 2*)

5 Duke of Exeter (*Scene 2*)

6 King Henry (*Scene 2*)

7 King Henry (*Scene 1*)

8 The Dauphin (*Scene 2*)

TEST YOURSELF (ACT II)

1 Chorus (*Chorus*)

2 Pistol (*Scene 1*)

3 King Henry (*Scene 2*)

4 Scroop (*Scene 2*)

5 The Dauphin (*Scene 4*)

6 Scroop (*Scene 2*)

7 Falstaff (*Scene 3*)

8 King Henry (*Scene 4*)

TEST YOURSELF (ACT III)

1 King Henry (*Scene 1*)

2 The Boy (*Scene 2*)

3 Fluellen (*Scene 2*)

4 Pistol (*Scene 6*)

5 King Henry (*Scene 6*)

6 The Dauphin (*Scene 7*)

7 Bardolph (*Scene 2*)

8 King Henry (*Scene 5*)

9 Pistol (*Scene 6*)

10 The Dauphin (*Scene 7*)

TEST YOURSELF (ACT IV)

1 Pistol (*Scene 1*)

2 Constable of France (*Scene 2*)

3 Westmorland (*Scene 3*)

4 King Henry (*Scene 3*)

5 The Dauphin (*Scene 5*)

6 Fluellen (*Scene 7*)

7 Montjoy (*Scene 7*)

8 King Henry (*Chorus*)

9 Pistol (*Scene 4*)

10 Duke of York (*Scene 6*)

TEST YOURSELF (ACT V)

1 Pistol (*Scene 1*)

2 Burgundy (*Scene 2*)

3 King Henry (*Scene 2*)

4 Queen of France (*Scene 2*)

5 King Henry (*Scene 2*)

6 Pistol (*Scene 1*)

7 Fluellen (*Scene 1*)

8 Princess Katherine (*Scene 2*)

Maya Angelou
I Know Why the Caged Bird Sings

Jane Austen
Pride and Prejudice

Alan Ayckbourn
Absent Friends

Elizabeth Barrett Browning
Selected Poems

Robert Bolt
A Man for All Seasons

Harold Brighouse
Hobson's Choice

Charlotte Brontë
Jane Eyre

Emily Brontë
Wuthering Heights

Shelagh Delaney
A Taste of Honey

Charles Dickens
David Copperfield
Great Expectations
Hard Times
Oliver Twist

Roddy Doyle
Paddy Clarke Ha Ha Ha

George Eliot
Silas Marner
The Mill on the Floss

Anne Frank
The Diary of a Young Girl

William Golding
Lord of the Flies

Oliver Goldsmith
She Stoops to Conquer

Willis Hall
The Long and the Short and the Tall

Thomas Hardy
Far from the Madding Crowd

The Mayor of Casterbridge
Tess of the d'Urbervilles
The Withered Arm and other Wessex Tales

L.P. Hartley
The Go-Between

Seamus Heaney
Selected Poems

Susan Hill
I'm the King of the Castle

Barry Hines
A Kestrel for a Knave

Louise Lawrence
Children of the Dust

Harper Lee
To Kill a Mockingbird

Laurie Lee
Cider with Rosie

Arthur Miller
The Crucible
A View from the Bridge

Robert O'Brien
Z for Zachariah

Frank O'Connor
My Oedipus Complex and Other Stories

George Orwell
Animal Farm

J.B. Priestley
An Inspector Calls
When We Are Married

Willy Russell
Educating Rita
Our Day Out

J.D. Salinger
The Catcher in the Rye

William Shakespeare
Henry IV Part I
Henry V
Julius Caesar
Macbeth

The Merchant of Venice
A Midsummer Night's Dream
Much Ado About Nothing
Romeo and Juliet
The Tempest
Twelfth Night

George Bernard Shaw
Pygmalion

Mary Shelley
Frankenstein

R.C. Sherriff
Journey's End

Rukshana Smith
Salt on the snow

John Steinbeck
Of Mice and Men

Robert Louis Stevenson
Dr Jekyll and Mr Hyde

Jonathan Swift
Gulliver's Travels

Robert Swindells
Daz 4 Zoe

Mildred D. Taylor
Roll of Thunder, Hear My Cry

Mark Twain
Huckleberry Finn

James Watson
Talking in Whispers

Edith Wharton
Ethan Frome

William Wordsworth
Selected Poems

A Choice of Poets

Mystery Stories of the Nineteenth Century including The Signalman

Nineteenth Century Short Stories

Poetry of the First World War

Six Women Poets

Margaret Atwood
Cat's Eye
The Handmaid's Tale

Jane Austen
Emma
Mansfield Park
Persuasion
Pride and Prejudice
Sense and Sensibility

Alan Bennett
Talking Heads

William Blake
Songs of Innocence and of Experience

Charlotte Brontë
Jane Eyre
Villette

Emily Brontë
Wuthering Heights

Angela Carter
Nights at the Circus

Geoffrey Chaucer
The Franklin's Prologue and Tale
The Miller's Prologue and Tale
The Prologue to the Canterbury Tales
The Wife of Bath's Prologue and Tale

Samuel Coleridge
Selected Poems

Joseph Conrad
Heart of Darkness

Daniel Defoe
Moll Flanders

Charles Dickens
Bleak House
Great Expectations
Hard Times

Emily Dickinson
Selected Poems

John Donne
Selected Poems

Carol Ann Duffy
Selected Poems

George Eliot
Middlemarch
The Mill on the Floss

T.S. Eliot
Selected Poems
The Waste Land

F. Scott Fitzgerald
The Great Gatsby

E.M. Forster
A Passage to India

Brian Friel
Translations

Thomas Hardy
Jude the Obscure
The Mayor of Casterbridge
The Return of the Native
Selected Poems
Tess of the d'Urbervilles

Seamus Heaney
Selected Poems from 'Opened Ground'

Nathaniel Hawthorne
The Scarlet Letter

Homer
The Iliad
The Odyssey

Aldous Huxley
Brave New World

Kazuo Ishiguro
The Remains of the Day

Ben Jonson
The Alchemist

James Joyce
Dubliners

John Keats
Selected Poems

Christopher Marlowe
Doctor Faustus
Edward II

Arthur Miller
Death of a Salesman

John Milton
Paradise Lost Books I & II

Toni Morrison
Beloved

George Orwell
Nineteen Eighty-Four

Sylvia Plath
Selected Poems

Alexander Pope
Rape of the Lock & Selected Poems

William Shakespeare
Antony and Cleopatra
As You Like It
Hamlet
Henry IV Part I
King Lear
Macbeth
Measure for Measure
The Merchant of Venice
A Midsummer Night's Dream
Much Ado About Nothing
Othello
Richard II
Richard III
Romeo and Juliet
The Taming of the Shrew
The Tempest
Twelfth Night
The Winter's Tale

George Bernard Shaw
Saint Joan

Mary Shelley
Frankenstein

Jonathan Swift
Gulliver's Travels and A Modest Proposal

Alfred Tennyson
Selected Poems

Virgil
The Aeneid

Alice Walker
The Color Purple

Oscar Wilde
The Importance of Being Earnest

Tennessee Williams
A Streetcar Named Desire

Jeanette Winterson
Oranges Are Not the Only Fruit

John Webster
The Duchess of Malfi

Virginia Woolf
To the Lighthouse

W.B. Yeats
Selected Poems

Metaphysical Poets

THE ULTIMATE WEB SITE FOR THE ULTIMATE LITERATURE GUIDES

At York Notes we believe in helping you achieve exam success. Log on to **www.yorknotes.com** and see how we have made revision even easier, with over 300 titles available to download twenty-four hours a day. The downloads have lots of additional features such as pop-up boxes providing instant glossary definitions, user-friendly links to every part of the guide, and scanned illustrations offering visual appeal. All you need to do is log on to **www.yorknotes.com** and download the books you need to help you achieve exam success.

KEY FEATURES:

Details on how York Notes can help you

Menu Bar to help you find your way around the site

Details on how to download York Notes

Quick Search facility to help you find the titles you need

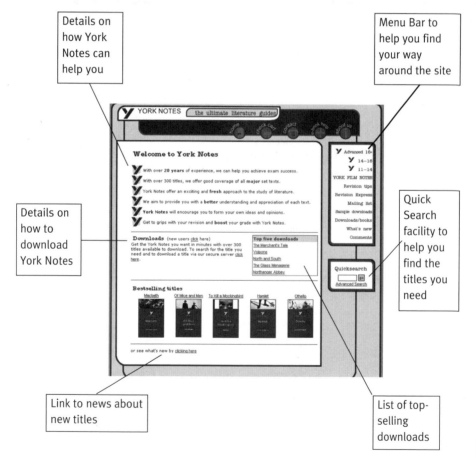

Link to news about new titles

List of top-selling downloads